OTHER BOOKS BY *Albert Camus*

Awarded the Nobel Prize for Literature in 1957

RESISTANCE, REBELLION, AND DEATH   *1961*
  (*Actuelles*—a selection)

THE POSSESSED (*Les Possédés*)   *1960*

CALIGULA AND THREE OTHER PLAYS   *1958*
  (*Caligula, Le Malentendu, L'État de siège, Les Justes*)

EXILE AND THE KINGDOM (*L'Exil et le Royaume*)   *1958*

THE FALL (*La Chute*)   *1957*

THE MYTH OF SISYPHUS AND OTHER ESSAYS   *1955*
  (*Le Mythe de Sisyphe*)

THE REBEL (*L'Homme révolté*)   *1954*

THE PLAGUE (*La Peste*)   *1948*

THE STRANGER (*L'Étranger*)   *1946*

These are BORZOI BOOKS,
published in New York by Alfred A. Knopf

NOTEBOOKS

1935 – 1942

NOTEBOOKS

1935 – 1942

By *Albert Camus*

TRANSLATED FROM THE FRENCH, AND
WITH A PREFACE AND NOTES, BY
PHILIP THODY

ALFRED A. KNOPF · *NEW YORK*

1963

L. C. catalog card number: 63–9127

THIS IS A BORZOI BOOK

PUBLISHED BY ALFRED A. KNOPF, INC.

FIRST AMERICAN EDITION

Originally published in French under the title Carnets, mai 1935–fevrier 1942. *© 1962, Editions Gallimard. Published in English in Great Britain under the title* Carnets 1935–1942 *by Hamish Hamilton Ltd.*

INTRODUCTION

IT WAS in May 1935, when he was twenty-two, that Albert Camus made the first entries in the literary diary which he continued to keep until his death in 1960. The entries were jotted down in a series of ordinary school exercise books, and were not originally intended for publication. In 1954, however, he had a typewritten copy made of the first seven notebooks, and corrected it with the obvious intention of eventually allowing these to be published. Extracts had already appeared in review form in both French and English when the complete edition of the first three *cahiers* was published in Paris in May 1962.[1] Camus's literary executors—Mme Albert Camus, M. René Char, and M. Jean Grenier—intend to publish the typescript of the next four of these notebooks, in two volumes, in the course of the next few years, but have not yet taken a decision about the notebooks for the period 1954–1960, which are still in manuscript form. The text here presented to English readers reproduces all the entries made in the original French edition, and will be followed by the translation of the next two volumes as they appear. This French edition, it should be noted, was given the title of

[1] The first publication of extracts from the notebooks was in *Symposium*, Spring–Fall 1958, pp. 1–7, while Camus was still alive. They consisted of his first draft for *The Plague*. Extracts appeared in the *Nouvelle Revue Française* in March 1962 and in a translation by Anthony Hartley in *Encounter*, October 1961, pp. 11–35.

Carnets. This was solely in order to avoid any possible confusion with the *Cahiers Albert Camus*, a series of critical essays on his work at present awaiting publication. Camus himself always referred to the notebooks as his *cahiers*.

When Camus was revising the typewritten copy in 1954, he underlined the fact that the notebooks were not to be looked upon as fragments of an autobiography by removing any passages that, in his view, dealt too directly with his own private feelings and experiences. There were, in any case, remarkably few of these, and it is significant that the *cahiers* for the period 1935–1942 did not contain any open reference either to his first or to his second marriage, and provided no details about his membership in the Communist Party or his work as a journalist on *Alger-Républicain*. As will be seen in later volumes, he did subsequently use the notebooks for more general purposes, but this was only because he felt that his memory was going. "Until this improves," he wrote in October 1946, "I must obviously note down more and more things here, even if they are personal"—a clear indication that, by allowing non-literary consideration to intrude, he was changing the original character of the *cahiers*.

This does not mean that the *Notebooks* are to be read merely as exercises in style, or that they show him to have actually been the "objective" writer [2] that he said he wanted to become. If they tell us relatively little about what he did, they are full of information about how he felt. His own political activity is not described, but a number of entries tell of his dislike of professional politicians, his horror at the outbreak of war in 1939, and his readiness to see a compromise peace achieved in the first year of the war. He gives no details about the different jobs which he took in order to earn a living, or about his other personal and emotional difficulties, but the honesty with which he mentions his horror of work and the

[2] Cf. *L'Eté*, 1954, p. 132. "I call an objective writer one who chooses subjects without ever taking himself as subject matter."

frequency with which he returns to the problem of loneliness do invite us to make a number of guesses about the kind of person he was. Yet it is first and foremost as a writer that Camus interests us, and for the light which the *Notebooks* throw on the way he worked that they are most valuable.

The entries made in the first volume can, from this point of view, be divided into three main categories. First of all, there are the philosophical ideas, the fragments of description, the scraps of conversation overheard at home or in the street, which Camus actually used in works published during his lifetime. To judge from the *cahiers* themselves, Camus often wrote passages that needed very little revision before being incorporated into the final version of his works. For example, both a number of extracts from *The Stranger* and several passages in the early essays *Noces* and *L'Envers et l'Endroit* were written straight out into the notebooks and underwent very few changes before being printed. The planning and organization [3] of his works always required a great deal of revision—there were seven versions of *The Fall,* possibly as many of *The Plague,* and at least two of *Caligula*—but the notebooks show Camus as a man who could, on occasion, "write without blotting a line." He also, it may be noted, made practically no stylistic changes in the later typewritten copy, and the published French text is not significantly different, either in style or content, from what he wrote down in the nineteen-forties. What Anthony Hartley referred to as the "bare, classical outline" of some of the phrases in the *Notebooks,* and what at least one French critic suggested might be the result of later revision, was a quality that came quite naturally to Camus at the very beginning of his career as a writer. The physical appearance of the notebooks, where a number of passages are written out in pencil and where the

[3] Cf. article by Roger Quilliot in *Démocratie,* January 4, 1962, and in *Le Figaro littéraire,* February 10, 1962. M. Quilliot observes, however, that *The Stranger* seems to have been written "quasiment d'un trait." For Anthony Hartley, cf. *Encounter,* October 1961, p. 11.

handwriting is most unlike that of a man copying from an earlier version, precludes any idea that the entries were the fruit of careful rewriting. What we have in the *cahiers* is French as Camus spontaneously wrote it.

The second of the two categories concerns some of the books which Camus read between 1935 and 1942. It is obvious at first glance, however, that he made notes on relatively few of these, and mentioned only some of the authors who made a particular impact on him. For example, not one of the works which he reviewed in *Alger-Républicain* in 1938 and 1939— and which included Sartre's *La Nausée* and *Le Mur*—is mentioned in the notebooks, and there are only passing references to other authors whose work he happened to review after coming to Paris in 1940. This fact, added to the frequency with which certain writers, especially Nietzsche, are quoted both in the notebooks and in Camus's published philosophical essays, is a further indication of the particular role which he assigned to his *cahiers*. They were not a record of everything that he had thought or read, but merely a place to note down some—but by no means all—of the themes, experiences, and ideas which he thought he might find useful. Quite a large number of these ideas did find their way into his published work, and the notes added to this translation are intended as a guide for readers interested in how they were then used. Thus one can see the essential themes of *The Stranger* and *The Myth of Sisyphus*—the finality of death, the immense value accorded to physical life and to intellectual lucidity, the rejection of any religious belief—occurring several years before the actual composition of the works, and developing in reaction to new experiences like travel and the outbreak of war. More particularly, an entry like the two quotations made from Tolstoy's *Confession* in 1942, after *The Myth of Sisyphus* had been completed, is a most interesting indication as to the way in which Camus's ideas were beginning to develop at that time.

As might be expected, the third and largest category is that of the entries which Camus did not finally use in his published work, and which are therefore interesting mainly as evidence of ambitions that he at one time entertained but subsequently abandoned. A number of them were, however, used in the early novel *La Mort Heureuse*,[4] on which Camus continued to work after he had had a typewritten copy made of the first draft between 1937 and 1938, and will therefore become easier to understand if his trustees finally allow this work to be published. In the meantime, the following brief account of the novel, based upon this typescript, will enable some of these entries to fall into context.

There are a number of resemblances between *La Mort Heureuse*, to which Camus may have been referring when he noted, on September 30, 1937, that it was "through a desire to shine too early that some authors did not agree to rewrite," and *The Stranger*, the novel that seems to have grown out of it and was published in 1942. Both novels are set in Algeria, and Patrice Mersault, the hero of *La Mort Heureuse*, shares a number of the characteristics of Meursault, the hero of *The Stranger*. Both seem to be only sons of widowed mothers, both are young men earning their living as clerks after having had to give up their studies, both enjoy living in Algeria, are fond of swimming, have a mistress, find nothing of interest to do on a Sunday, and tend to fall asleep as soon as work or physical pleasure leave a gap in their lives. Patrice Mersault, however —as can be gathered from the entries in the *Notebooks*—has

[4] The typescript of *La Mort Heureuse* which I was allowed to read was dated 1937–1938, and M. Quilliot tells me that he has discovered no reason to doubt the accuracy of these dates. There is, however, another manuscript in existence, which may in fact contain all the corrections made after 1937. As will be seen from the *Notebooks*, Camus stated his intention of revising this novel in June 1938, and was still experimenting with a new style of narration as late as March 1939.

The *Pléiade* edition of Camus's novels and plays, which M. Quilliot is at the moment preparing, will contain short extracts illustrating the similarities and differences between *La Mort Heureuse* and *The Stranger*.

a more deliberate interest in achieving conscious happiness than the easygoing Meursault, and the novel opens with his killing, apparently with his victim's consent, a rich but almost completely paralyzed invalid called Zagreus. The aim of the murder is to provide Mersault with enough money to pursue his quest for happiness unhindered by poverty or the need to earn a living.

Mersault then sets out on a long journey in Eastern Europe —fragments of Camus's description of this in the novel are in the *Notebooks* and were later incorporated into one of the essays in *L'Envers et l'Endroit*—but soon returns to Algeria, with the chill that he caught on the evening of Zagreus's murder developing into something more serious. After a brief stay with some of his friends in the Maison devant le Monde [5] —the description of this episode is perhaps the most openly autobiographical passage in the whole of Camus's work—he marries and goes to live in a small village on the Algerian coast near the ruins of Tipasa. There, after an imprudent midnight swim, his illness grows worse and he dies, fully conscious at the very moment of his death of everything that is happening to him. The second part of the novel is called, appropriately enough, *La Mort Consciente* (*Conscious Death*), and the Pantheistic harmony with the rest of creation that Mersault feels on his deathbed thereby justifies its general title.

Different views have been expressed about the value of *La Mort Heureuse*—the reader will find another account of it in Germaine Brée's book on Camus—and it is certainly not as perfectly finished a work as *The Stranger*. Its very defects, however—a certain diffuseness and lack of construction, too obvious a use of personal experiences—enable us to understand why Camus never submitted it to a publisher, and proceeded to write *The Stranger,* a work which he was later

[5] A description of the Maison devant le Monde can be found in Germaine Brée's book.

to call an "exercise in objectivity." One of the most interesting opportunities which the *Notebooks* offer us is that of seeing something of how this was done, and of watching an author both creating a new work and reflecting critically on the principles which must guide this creation. One of the many stories to be read between the lines of these *Notebooks* is that of the struggle between Camus's intellectual recognition of the need for discipline and what he referred to, in an interview in 1959, as the "profound anarchy" [6] of his temperament.

The pleasure which I have taken in translating and editing the *Notebooks* has been redoubled by Mme Camus's generosity in allowing me access to the original *cahiers*, to the unpublished typescript copy for the period 1942–1954, and to the typescript of *La Mort Heureuse*. I should like to take this opportunity of expressing my gratitude for all the help which she has given me.

Philip Thody

[6] Cf. interview in Claude Brisville's study in *La Bibliothèque idéale*, Gallimard, 1959, p. 258. Camus also remarked, however: "I make myself strict rules in order to correct my nature. But it is my nature that I finally obey. The result is far from brilliant." In the same interview, he described his manner of working as: "Notes, scraps of paper, reverie, which all might go on for years. Then, one day, I have the idea or conception that makes all these isolated fragments coagulate together. There then begins a long and painful putting them into order."

CONTENTS

NOTEBOOK I

May 1935 – September 1937

MAY 1935

What I mean is this: that one can, with no romanticism, feel nostalgic for lost poverty. A certain number of years lived without money are enough to create a whole sensibility. In this particular case, the strange feeling which the son has for his mother constitutes his whole sensibility. The latent material memory which he has of his childhood (a glue that has stuck to the soul) explains why this way of feeling shows itself in the most widely differing fields.

Whoever notices this in himself feels both gratitude and a guilty conscience. If he has moved into a different class, the comparison also gives him the feeling that he has lost great wealth. For rich people, the sky is just an extra, a

3

gift of nature. The poor, on the other hand, can see it as it really is: an infinite grace.[1]

A guilty conscience needs to confess. A work of art is a confession, and I must bear witness. When I see things clearly, I have only one thing to say. It is in this life of poverty, among these vain or humble people, that I have most certainly touched what I feel is the true meaning of life. Works of art will never provide this and art is not everything for me. Let it at least be a means.

What also count are the small acts of cowardice, the times one is ashamed, the way one thinks of the other world, the world of money, without being aware of doing so. I think that the world of the poor is one of the few, if not the only one, which is wholly turned in upon itself, so that it forms an island in society. It is quite cheap to go there and play at being Robinson Crusoe. But someone who has dived down right into it has to say "over there" when talking about the doctor's house next door.

All this must be expressed through a study of the mother and the son.

What I have just written applies to things in general.

[1] This is repeated, in slightly different form, in Camus's first volume of essays, *L'Envers et l'Endroit*, first published in Algiers in 1937. All references here, however, are to the 1958 Gallimard edition. An English translation of these essays is in preparation. Cf. p. 63: "At a certain level of wealth, the sky itself and the star-filled sky seem natural goods. But at the bottom of the scale, the sky recovers all its meaning: a priceless gift of grace.

The mother-son relationship recurs in *The Stranger, The Plague*, and *The Misunderstanding*. Camus loved his mother intensely, and wrote in a later *cahier*, in 1952: "When my mother's eyes were not resting on me, I have never been able to look at her without tears springing into my eyes." For a further analysis of the name and relationship pattern in Camus's work, cf. Carl A. Viggiani: "Camus' *L'Etranger*," in PMLA, December 1956.

When one comes down to particular instances, everything becomes more complicated.

(1) A setting. A neighborhood and its inhabitants.

(2) The mother and what she does.

(3) The relationship between the son and his mother.

What is the solution? The mother? End with a chapter describing how her symbolic value comes into being through the son's nostalgia?

Grenier: [2] We always have too low an opinion of ourselves. But in poverty, illness, or loneliness we become aware of our eternity. "We need to be forced into our very last bastions."

That's exactly it, neither more nor less.

Vanity of the word *experience*. You cannot acquire experience by making experiments. You cannot create experience. You must undergo it. Patience rather than experience. We wait patiently—or, rather, we are patients.

It is all practice: when we emerge from experience we are not wise but skillful. But at what?

Two women, close friends, both very ill. But one with a nervous complaint and capable of recovery. The other in the last stages of consumption. No hope.

[2] Jean Grenier, a philosopher in his own right, was Camus's philosophy teacher in Algiers and exercised a considerable influence over his thought. Both *L'Envers et l'Endroit* and *The Rebel* are dedicated to him. For more details, cf. my own study *Albert Camus 1913–1960* (The Macmillan Company, 1961), pp. 235–6.

One afternoon the consumptive at her friend's bed-side. The latter:

"Up to now, you see, even in my worst attacks, I still had something. A stubborn hope to keep alive. Now, I feel there is nothing left to hope for. I'm so tired that I feel I shall never get up again."

Her friend, a fierce joy shining in her eyes, took her hand:

"Oh, we shall make the great voyage together."

They were both the same—the one dying, the other almost cured. She had gone to France especially to try out a new treatment.

And the other blames her for it. She seems to be reproaching her friend for leaving her behind. In fact, the sight of her friend getting better makes her suffer. She had had this mad hope of not dying alone, of taking her dearest friend with her. Now she is going to die alone. And this knowledge feeds her friendship with a terrible hatred.

Storm sky in August. Gusts of hot wind. Black clouds. Yet in the East a delicate, transparent band of blue sky. Impossible to look at it. Its presence is a torture for the eyes and for the soul, because beauty is unbearable, drives us to despair, offering us for a minute the glimpse of an eternity that we should like to stretch out over the whole of time.

He is at ease in sincerity. Very rare.

The theme of comedy is also important. What saves us from our worst suffering is the feeling that we are abandoned and alone, and yet not sufficiently alone for "other people" to stop "sympathizing with us" in our unhappiness. It is in this sense that our moments of happiness are often those when we are lifted up into an endless sadness by the feeling that everyone has forsaken us. Also in this sense that happiness is often only the self-pitying awareness of our unhappiness.

This is very noticeable among the poor—God put self-pity by the side of despair like the cure by the side of the disease.

When I was young, I expected people to give me more than they could—continuous friendship, permanent emotion.

Now I have learned to expect less of them than they can give—a silent companionship. And their emotions, their friendship, and noble gestures keep their full miraculous value in my eyes; wholly the fruit of grace.

They had already had too much to drink and wanted a meal. But it was Christmas Eve and the restaurant was full. They were turned away, but had insisted and were thrown out. They had then kicked the owner's wife, who was pregnant. The owner, a frail, fair-haired young man, had taken a gun and opened fire. The bullet had lodged in the man's right temple. His head had now rolled over and was resting on the wound. Drunk with alcohol and terror, his friend had begun to dance around his body.

What had happened was quite straightforward, and would all end up tomorrow in the newspaper. But, for the moment, in this out of the way corner, the sight of the pavement glistening under the occasional street lamp after the recent rain, the long, wet hissing of the tires of passing cars, the brightly lit streetcars clanging back from time to time, gave this scene sprung from another world a disquieting relief: the sweetly sickening and insistent image that the neighborhood takes on when night peoples its streets with shadows—or, rather, when one single anonymous shadow, heralded by a dull movement of feet, sometimes leaps forward, bathed in crimson glory, in the red light cast by the bulb outside a pharmacy.

JANUARY 1936 [3]

Beyond the window there is a garden, but I can see only its walls. And a few branches flowing with light. A little higher, I see more branches, and higher still the sun. And of all the jubilation of the air that can be felt outdoors, of all that joy spread out over the world, I can see only shadows of branches playing on white curtains. There are also five rays of sunlight patiently pouring into the room the white scent of dried grass. A breeze, and the shadows on the curtains come to life. If a cloud covers up the sun and then lets it through again, the bright yellow of the vase of mimosa leaps out of the shade. The birth of this single flash of brightness is enough to fill me with a confused and whirling joy.

[3] This description, later incorporated with minor changes into *L'Envers et l'Endroit*, pp. 121–4, was written straight out into the Notebooks with very few alterations or corrections.

A prisoner in the cave, I lie alone and look at the shadow of the world. A January afternoon. But the heart of the air is full of cold. Everywhere a thin film of sunlight that you could split with a touch of your fingernail, but which clothes everything in an eternal smile. Who am I and what can I do—except enter into the movement of the branches and the light, be this ray of sunlight in which my cigarette smolders away, this soft and gentle passion breathing in the air? If I try to reach myself, it is at the heart of this light that I am to be found. And if I try to taste and understand this delicate flavor that contains the secret of the world, it is again myself that I find at the heart of the universe. Myself, that is to say this intense emotion which frees me from my surroundings. Soon, my attention will be filled again with other things and with the world of men. But let me cut out this moment from the cloth of time as other men leave a flower in the pages of a book. In it, they enclose the memory of a walk in which they were touched by love. I also walk through the world, but am caressed by a god. Life is short, and it is a sin to waste one's time. I waste my time all day long, while other people say that I do a great deal. Today is a resting place, and my heart goes out to meet itself.

If I still feel a grain of anxiety, it is at the thought of this unseizable moment slipping through my fingers like a ball of quicksilver. Let those who want to, stand aside from the world. I no longer feel sorry for myself, for now I see myself being born. I am happy in this world for my kingdom is of this world. A cloud passes and a moment grows pale. I die to myself. The book opens at a well-loved page—how tasteless it is when compared to the book of the world. Is it true that I have suffered, is it not true that I am suffering? And that I am drunk with this suffering because it is made up of that sun and these shadows, of this warmth and that coldness which can be felt afar off, at the very heart of the air? What cause to wonder if something dies or men suffer, when everything is written on this window where the sun pours forth its fullness? I can say, and in a moment I shall say, that what counts is to be true, and then everything fits in, both humanity and simplicity. And when am I truer and more transparent than when I *am* the world?

Moment of adorable silence. But the song of the world rises and I, a prisoner chained deep in the cave, am filled with delight before I have time to desire. Eternity is here while I was waiting for it. Now I can speak. I do not know what I could wish for rather than this continued presence of self with self. What I want now is not happiness but awareness. One thinks one has cut oneself off from the world, but it is enough to see an olive tree upright in the golden dust, or beaches glistening in the morning sun, to feel this separation melt away. Thus with me. I became aware of the possibilities for which I am responsible. Every minute of life carries with it its miraculous value, and its face of eternal youth.

People can think only in images. If you want to be a philosopher, write novels.[4]

[4] Importance of images in fiction—an idea repeated in *L'Envers et l'Endroit,* pp. 72–3, and in *The Myth of Sisyphus.* Cf. English translation by Justin O'Brien (Alfred A. Knopf, 1955), p. 100. It also occurs in Camus's review of *La Nausée* in *Alger-Républicain* on October 20,

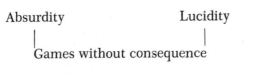

May 1935 – September 1937

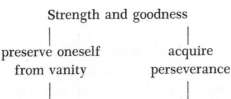

Absurdity   Lucidity

Games without consequence

Strength and goodness

preserve oneself   acquire
from vanity   perseverance

A Saint: Keep silent. Act. Socialism
Acquisition and achievement.

Basically: heroic values.

PART II [5]

A. In the present
B. In the past

Ch. A1—The House before the World. Introduction.
Ch. B1—Memories. Affair with Lucienne.
Ch. A2—House before the World. His youth.
Ch. B2—Lucienne tells of her acts of infidelity.
Ch. A3—House before the World. Invitation.

1938. "A novel is never anything but a philosophy put into images. And in a good novel, the whole of the philosophy has passed into the images." *La Nausée*, in his view, did not wholly satisfy this criterion.

[5] This list of contents seems to be a first draft for *La Mort Heureuse*. The House before the World was an actual house overlooking the sea, on the outskirts of Algiers, which Camus shared with a number of other students in the nineteen-thirties. It is described in *La Mort Heureuse*. There, Mersault is jealous of an affair which one of his mistresses, Marthe, had had with another man. He eventually marries Lucienne.

Patrice tells his story of the man sentenced to death: [6]
"I can see him, he is inside me. And everything he says
pierces my heart. He lives and breathes with me. He is
afraid with me.

". . . And the other man who tries to break down his
resistance. I can see him living too. He is in me. I send
him the priest every day to weaken him.

"I know that now I am going to write. There comes a
time when the tree, after much suffering, must bear fruit.
Every winter ends in a spring. I must bear witness.
Afterwards, the cycle will start up again.

"I shall tell of nothing but my love of life. But I shall tell
of it in my own way. . . .

"Others write because of the temptations they have put
off. And each disappointment in life makes a work of art
for them, a lie woven out of the lies of their life. But what
I write will spring from my moments of happiness, even

[6] It is interesting to see the theme of capital punishment occurring
so early. It was one of the main preoccupations of Camus's life; it
formed the subject matter of *The Stranger* and *The Plague*, inspired
the *Reflections on the Guillotine*, cf. *Resistance, Rebellion, and Death*
(Alfred A. Knopf, 1960), pp. 173–234, and lay at the basis of many of
his political attitudes.

Patrice is Mersault's Christian name in *La Mort Heureuse*. The theme
of the man sentenced to death hardly appears at all in the "final"
(1937–1938) version of *La Mort Heureuse*. It is, of course, at the very
centre of *The Stranger*.

when what I write is cruel. I must write as I must swim, because my body demands it."

PART III (all in the present)

Chapt. I—"Catherine," says Patrice, "I know that now I am going to write. The story of the condemned man. I have come back to my real function, which is to write."
Chapt. II—Descent from the House before the World to the port, etc. Taste of death and of the sun. Love of life.

Six stories:
The story of the brilliant game. Luxury.
The story of the poor neighborhood. Death of the mother.
The story of the House before the World.
The story of sexual jealousy.
The story of the condemned man.
The story of the descent toward the sun.

In the Balearic Islands. Last summer [7]
What gives value to travel is fear. It is the fact that, at a certain moment, when we are so far from our own country (a French newspaper acquires incalculable value. And

[7] These reflections on travel recur, in slightly changed form, in *L'Envers et l'Endroit,* pp. 108–9, when Camus is describing his visit to Palma.

those evenings when, in cafés, you try to get close to other men just to touch them with your elbow), we are seized by a vague fear, and an instinctive desire to go back to the protection of old habits. This is the most obvious benefit of travel. At that moment we are feverish but also porous, so that the slightest touch makes us quiver to the depths of our being. We come across a cascade of light, and there is eternity. This is why we should not say that we travel for pleasure. There is no pleasure in traveling, and I look upon it more as an occasion for spiritual testing. If we understand by culture the exercise of our most intimate sense—that of eternity—then we travel for culture. Pleasure takes us away from ourselves in the same way as distraction, in Pascal's use of the word, takes us away from God. Travel, which is like a greater and a graver science, brings us back to ourselves.

The Balearic Islands
   The bay.
   San Francisco—the cloister.
   Bellver.
   The wealthy district (the shadows and the old
      women).
   The poor district (the window).
   The cathedral (bad taste and a masterpiece).
   A café with a piano.
   The coast of Miramar.
   Valldemosa and the terraces.
   Soller and midday.
   San Antonio (convent). Felanitx.

Pollensa: the town. The convent. The boarding-house.

Ibiza: the bay.

La Peña: the fortifications.

San Eulalia: the beach. The festival.

The cafés around the port.

The stone walls and the windmills in the country.

FEBRUARY 13, 1936

I ask of people more than they can give me. It is useless to maintain the contrary. But what a mistake and what despair. And myself perhaps. . . .

Seek contacts. All contacts. If I want to write about men, should I stop talking about the countryside? If the sky or light attract me, shall I forget the eyes or voices of those I love? Each time I am given the elements of a friendship, the fragments of an emotion, never the emotion or the friendship itself.

You go to see an older friend to tell him everything. Or, at least, something which is stifling you. But he is in a hurry. You talk about everything and about nothing at all. The time to speak has gone. And here I am, more alone and empty than before. How a careless word from a friend escaping from my presence will lay waste this feeble wisdom that I am trying to construct! "Non ridere, non lugere" . . . and doubts about myself and about other people.

MARCH

A day of sunshine and clouds. The cold spangled with yellow. I ought to keep a diary of each day's weather. The fine, transparent sunshine yesterday. The bay trembling with light like a moist lip.[8] And I have worked all day.

A title: The hope of the world.

Grenier on Communism: "The whole question comes down to this: should one, for an ideal of justice, accept stupid ideas?" One can reply "yes," this is a fine thing to do. Or "no," it is honest to refuse.

With a due sense of proportion, one can see the same problem here as in Christianity. Should the believer load himself down with the contradictions in the Gospels and the excesses of the Church? Does believing in Christianity involve accepting Noah's ark and defending the Inquisition? or the tribunal which condemned Galileo?

But, on the other hand, how can we reconcile Communism and disgust? If I try extreme forms of action, in so far as they reach absurdity and uselessness—then I reject Communism. And this concern for religious matters. . . .

It is death which gives gambling and heroism their true meaning.

[8] The image of the bay like a moist lip occurs again in *L'Envers et l'Endroit*, p. 54.

Yesterday. The sun on the quays, the Arab acrobats, and the port leaping with light. It is as if, for the last winter [9] that I shall spend here, this country were offering me all its riches. This unique winter, glistening with cold and sunlight. Blue cold.

Lucid ecstasy and smiling destitution—the despair which we see in the virile acceptance reflected in Greek stelae. Why do I need to write or create, to love or suffer? The part of my life which is now lost is not, basically, the most important. Everything becomes pointless.

Neither despair nor joy seems justified before this sky and the shining suffocating heat pouring down from it.

MAY 16

A long walk. Hills with the sea in the background. And the delicate sun. White eglantines in all the bushes. Heavy, syrupy flowers with violet-colored petals. Also the return home, gentleness and friendship of women. Grave and smiling faces of young women. Smiles, jokes, and plans. One goes back into the game. And, without believing in them, everyone smiles at appearances and pretends to accept them. No false notes. I am linked to the world by

[9] Perhaps he had been told that his illness made it necessary for him to leave Algiers. Cf. entry on p. 44.

This entry, with its "tout devient inutile," foreshadowing something of the feeling of the absurdity of the world expressed in *The Stranger* and *The Myth of Sisyphus*, supports the views of those critics who see Camus's early work as strongly marked by his reaction to tuberculosis. He first fell ill in 1930, and never seems to have been completely cured, since he had relapses in 1936, 1942, and 1949. The tone here is almost that of a man seeking some consolation for a fate which he knows is inevitable and which he detests.

everything I do, to men with all the gratitude I feel.[1] From the hilltop, we could see the mists left by the recent rains being pressed down and brought back to life by the sun. Even as I came down through the woods, diving down into this cotton wool, I sensed the sun above me and saw the trees appearing one by one in this miraculous daylight. Trust and friendship, sun and white houses, scarcely grasped shades of meaning—oh, my untouched moments of happiness are already drifting away and offering no more help in the gloom of the evening than a young woman's smile or the understanding glance of shared friendship.

If time seems to pass so quickly, this is because there are no landmarks. Like the moon when it is at its height or on the horizon. The years of our youth are so long because they are so full, the years of our old age so short because each stage is already marked out. Note, for instance, that it is so interminable and exasperating to watch the

---

[1] A reflection which recurs in *L'Envers et l'Endroit*, p. 124, and provides one of the explanations for the idea of the "two sides of the coin" expressed in the title. As a number of other entries in the *Notebooks* show, Camus feels himself torn between a love for his fellow creatures and an ability to forget them in an instinctive communion with the world. This feeling of duality between men and the world persisted in one form or another throughout his work, and inspired the title of Roger Quilliot's study *La Mer et Les Prisons* in 1955. In an essay entitled *Return to Tipasa*, written in 1952 and included in *L'Eté* (translated in *The Myth of Sisyphus*, 1955), Camus wrote: "Yes, there is beauty and there are men suffering in humiliation. However difficult it may be, I should like never to be unfaithful either to the one or to the others" (*The Myth of Sisyphus*, p. 203). In his spoken introduction to recordings from his work (Disques *Festival*, FLD 25, ed. Gallimard, no date), Camus changed this to: "Whatever may be my defects as a man or as a writer. . . ."

hand turn for five minutes on a clock face that it is almost impossible to do so.[2]

MARCH

A gray sky, but with the light filtering through. In a moment there will be a few drops of rain. Down there, the bay was already looming through the mist. Happiness and those who are happy. They have only what they deserve.

MARCH

My joy is endless.

Dolorem exprimit quia movit amorem.

MARCH

A mental hospital above Algiers. A stiffish breeze, moving the grass and sunlight, climbs the hill. And all this white and tender movement comes to a halt some way from the summit, at the foot of the dark cypress trees, which then climb to the top in close-set ranks. An admirable light falling from the heavens. Below, no wrinkles on the smooth face of the sea smiling with its blue teeth. Upright in the wind, the sun warming one side of my face, I stand speechless as I watch this unique moment flow past me. But a patient arrives with his nurse, a box under

---

[2] Valentin, the hero of Queneau's novel *Le Dimanche de la Vie*, makes a similar discovery. Gallimard, 1951, p. 199.

his arm, and comes up to me with a serious expression on his face.

"Good morning, Mademoiselle" (this to the young woman with me). "Allow me to introduce myself. Monsieur Ambrosino."

"Monsieur Camus."

"Ah, now, I knew a Camou. Trucking business at Mostaganem. Must be one of your relatives."

"No."

"Doesn't matter. Let me stay with you a minute. I am allowed to go out for half an hour every day. But I have to grovel in front of the nurse to make him come with me. You one of this young lady's relatives?"

"No."

"In that case then, I'll tell you: we're going to get engaged at Easter. My wife says I can. Mademoiselle, pray accept these few flowers. This letter is for you as well. Sit down next to me. I only have half an hour."

"We must be going."

"Oh, all right, when shall I see you again?"

"Tomorrow."

"Ah. Well, you see, I only have half an hour and I came to play a little music."

We leave. On the road, we pass the magnificent bright color of the red geraniums. The patient has taken from his box a reed with a long split down the middle, covered over with a piece of rubber. He makes it produce a strange, plaintive, warm music: "Il pleut sur la route. . . ." The music follows us down past the great clumps of daisies, against the unruffled smile of the sea.

I open the letter. It contains advertisements cut out of

newspapers and carefully arranged with a number penciled on each.

M ³——Every day he used to put the gun on the table. When he had finished work, he would put his papers in order, put his head close to the revolver, place his forehead against it, roll his temples on it, cooling his hot, feverish cheeks against the cool metal. Then, for a long time, he would let his fingers wander along the trigger, playing with the safety catch, until the world grew silent about him, and, already half asleep, his whole being huddled down into the one sensation of this cold and salty metal from which could spring death.

As soon as one does not kill oneself, one must keep silent about life. And, as he woke up, his mouth filled with an already bitter saliva, he licked the barrel, poking his tongue into it, and with a death rattle of infinite happiness said again and again in wonder and astonishment: "My joy is priceless."

M—PART II

The successive catastrophes—his courage—life made up of these misfortunes. He settles down into the painful cloth from which his life is woven, builds up his days

³ A passage used in *La Mort Heureuse*. (The *cahiers* themselves, it may be noted, do not contain either the name Mersault or the different spelling of Meursault. The typescript, perhaps on Camus's instructions, renders most of the entries M. as Mersault.) The passage is, in fact, used to describe the invalid whom Mersault finally kills, Roland Zagreus. This passage, like the preceding one, was written straight out into the *Notebooks* without any alterations.

around his loneliness, his return home in the evening, his suspicion and disgust. People think he is tough and stoical. Really, things seem to be going quite well. One day, an insignificant incident: one of his friends speaks to him in an offhand manner. He goes home. Kills himself.[4]

I seem to be gradually emerging.
The gentle and restrained friendship of women.

The social question is now settled, and I have found my balance again. In a fortnight's time, I shall decide where I am. Think of my book all the time. From Sunday onwards, immediately start to organize my work.

I must start to build again after this long period of anguish and despair. Finally the sun and my panting body. Keep silent—and have confidence in myself.

APRIL

The first hot days of the year. Stifling. All the animals are lying on their side. At dusk, the air above the town takes on a strange quality. Noises rise and are lost in the air like balloons. Trees and men stand motionless. On the terrace of their houses, the Arab women gossip while waiting for evening to fall. The smell of coffee being roasted also rises in the air. An hour of tenderness and despair,

[4] The idea of a suicide caused by a moment of indifference occurs both in *L'Envers et l'Endroit*, p. 71, and in *The Myth of Sisyphus*, p. 5.

with nothing to embrace, nothing at whose feet to throw oneself, overcome with gratitude.

The heat on the quays—it crushes you with its enormous weight and takes away your breath. The thick and heavy smell of tar rasping in your throat. Annihilation and the taste of death. It is this which is the real climate of tragedy and not, as people usually consider, the night.

Sensations and the world—a mingling of desires. And in this body which I keep close to my own, I hold this strange joy which comes down from sky to sea.

Death and blood.[5] The docker with a broken leg. The drops of blood, falling one by one on the hot stones of the quay, sizzle and shrivel up. In the café, he tells me the story of his life. The others have gone. Six glasses stand on the table. He lived alone, in a small house in the suburbs, going home only in the evening to do the cooking. A dog, a tom and a female cat, six kittens, which the cat cannot feed. They die one by one. Every evening, a stiff dead body and filth. Two smells: death and urine mingling together. On the last evening (he stretches his arms across the table, wider and wider apart, slowly and gently pushing the glasses toward the edge) the last kitten died. But the mother had eaten half of it—half a cat left, as you

[5] A fragment reproduced in *La Mort Heureuse*. The story of the cats is also told, in the first person, in *L'Envers et l'Endroit*, pp. 71–2.

might say. And still all the filth. The wind howling around the house. A piano, in the far distance. He sat in the middle of these ruins and wretchedness. And the whole meaning of the world had suddenly surged up into his mouth. (One by one, the glasses fall from the table, as he stretches his arms wider and wider apart.) He stayed there for a long time, shaking with a vast, wordless anger, his head in his hands and the thought that he had got to get his dinner ready.

All the glasses are broken. And he smiles. "O.K.," he says to the owner, "I'll pay for everything."

The docker's broken leg. In a corner, a young man laughs silently to himself.

"It's nothing. What hurt most were general ideas." Running after the truck, speed, dust, and din. The wild rhythm of windlasses and machines, the masts dancing on the horizon, the hulls of the vessels lurching from side to side. And in the white, chalky dust, in the sun and blood, against the immense and fantastic background of the port, two young men being carried swiftly away, breathless with laughter as if overcome with dizziness.[6]

---

[6] This description was reproduced in the typescript of *La Mort Heureuse* and also recurs, with some changes, in *The Stranger*, p. 31. The character of Emmanuel also occurs in both novels, as Mersault's and Meursault's friend.

M A Y

One must not cut oneself off from the world. No one who lives in the sunlight makes a failure of his life. My whole effort, whatever the situation, misfortune or disillusion, must be to make contact again. But even within this sadness I feel a great leap of joy and a great desire to love simply at the sight of a hill against the evening sky.

Contacts with truth, with nature first of all, and then with the art of those who have understood and with my own art if I am capable of it. Otherwise, the sea, sunshine and delight, with the moist lips of desire, will simply lie there in front of me.

Smiling despair. No solution, but constantly exercising an authority over myself that I know is useless. The essential thing is not to lose oneself, and not to lose that part of oneself that lies sleeping in the world.

M A Y

All contacts—does this mean the Cult of the Self? [7] No. The Cult of the Self presupposes either optimism or a

[7] A probable reference to the trilogy entitled *Le Culte du Moi*, 1888–1891, by Maurice Barrès, a standard work of egocentric dilettantism. Camus wrote an article on Barrès in *La Lumière*, a very left-wing Parisian weekly, on April 5, 1940, in which he stated: "In his way, which was quite moving at times, Barrès was the aesthete of patriotism as he was the aesthete of individualism." The meaning of Camus's remarks in the *Notebooks* seems to be that, for someone like himself, who has not the time and leisure to "cultivate the self" in the way that Barrès's hero did, the correct attitude is one of constant attention to the different possibilities which day-to-day life contains. This idea recurs in *The Myth of Sisyphus*, p. 68: "A subclerk in the post office is the equal of a conqueror if consciousness is common to them."

dilettante's attitude toward life. Both nonsense. Do not select a life, but make the one you have stretch out.

Attention: for Kierkegaard, the origin of our suffering lies in comparisons.

Commit yourself completely. Then, show equal strength in accepting both yes and no.

MAY

These early evenings in Algiers when the women are so beautiful.

MAY

On the very edge—and over the edge lies a gambler's attitude [8] to life. I deny, I am cowardly and weak, I act as if I were saying yes, as if I were strong and brave. Question of will power—carry absurdity through to the very end—I am capable of. . . .

Hence, take this gambler's attitude tragically, as far as the effort one makes is concerned, but see it as comic (or, rather, as unimportant) in the result obtained.

But to do this, don't waste time. Look for the extreme experience in solitude. Purify gambling with your life by conquering yourself—knowing such conquest to be absurd.

Bring together the Hindu sage and the Western hero.

[8] Camus was fascinated by the words *jeu, jouer,* and *joueur,* with their different associations with gambling, sports, and play-acting, and deliberately exploited their ambiguity. This makes any translation an interpretation based on context.

"It is general ideas that hurt most."

This extreme experience must always come to an end before an outstretched hand. To be resumed later. Outstretched hands are rare.

God—the Mediterranean: constructions—nothing natural.

Nature = equivalence.

Against relapse and weakness: effort. Be careful of the demon:

culture—the body

the will—work (Phil.)

But the counterpart: the intercessors—every day

my work (emotions)

extreme experiences.

Philosophical work: absurdity.

Literary work: strength, love, and death under the sign of conquest.

In both, mingle the two styles while respecting the particular tone of each. One day, write a book that will give the meaning.

And show no emotion about this tension—despise comparisons.

An essay on death and on Philosophy—Malraux. India.

An essay on chemistry.

MAY

That life is the strongest force—true. But the starting point of all kinds of cowardice. We must make a point of thinking the opposite.

And now they start to bellow that I am immoral.

They must be translated as meaning that I need to give myself a morality. Admit it then, you fool. I do.

Another way of looking at it: you must be simple, truthful, not go in for literary declamations—accept and commit yourself. But we do nothing else.

If you are convinced of your despair, you must either act as if you did hope after all—or kill yourself. Suffering gives no rights.

An intellectual? Yes. And never deny it. An intellectual is someone whose mind watches itself. I like this, because I am happy to be both halves, the watcher and the watched. "Can they be brought together?" This is a practical question. We must get down to it. "I despise intelligence" really means: "I cannot bear my doubts."

I prefer to keep my eyes open.

NOVEMBER [9]

See Greece. Mind and feeling, a taste for *expression* as evidence of decadence. Greek sculpture starts to decline as

---

[9] Camus had to cancel his trip to Greece in 1939 because of the outbreak of war. He finally went there in 1955.

soon as the statues begin to smile and have an expression in their eyes. The same is true of Italian painting, with the "colorists" of the sixteenth century.

The paradox of the Greeks who are great artists in spite of themselves. The Doric Apollos are admirable because their faces are expressionless. Unfortunately, however, the way they were painted did actually give them an expression. But now that the paint has gone, the masterpiece remains.

Nationalities appear as signs of disintegration. Almost as soon as the religious unity of the Holy Roman Empire had been broken, nationalisms began to make themselves felt. In the East, we still find unity.

Internationalism is trying to restore to the West its true meaning and vocation. But this internationalism is based not on Christian but on Greek principles. Modern humanism deepens the gulf separating East and West—as in the case of Malraux. But it restores strength.

Protestantism. Nuance. In theory, Luther's and Kierkegaard's attitudes are admirable. In practice?

JANUARY

Caligula [1] or the meaning of death. 4 acts.

   I—(a) His accession. Joy. Virtuous speeches. (Cf. Suetonius.)

      (b) Mirror.

[1] As Germaine Brée has shown (*Symposium*, Spring–Fall 1958, pp. 43–8), the first version of *Caligula* was completed in 1938.

II—(a) His sisters and Drusilla.

    (b) Scorn for the great.

    (c) Death of Drusilla. Flight of Caligula.

III—

End: Caligula comes forward, drawing back the curtain:

"No, Caligula is not dead. He is there, and there. He is in each one of you. If you were given the power, if you had the courage, if you loved life, you would see this monster or this angel that you carry within yourselves break loose. Our century is dying for having accepted values, for having believed that things could be made beautiful and cease to be absurd. Farewell. I am going back into history, where those who are afraid to love too much have held me prisoner for so long."

JANUARY

Essay: The House before the World.

—In the neighborhood, people called it the house of the three Students.

—When you leave, it is to shut yourself away.

—The house before the world is not a house where you have a good time, but where you are happy.

"There are other people here besides well-brought-up young ladies," says M., in whose presence X is using bad language.

M. and love:

"You have reached the age where one is happy to recognize oneself in somebody else's child."

"You have to teach her Einstein's theory of relativity in order to make love."

"Heaven preserve us," says M.

The path up there is so steep that it is a conquest every time you climb it.

FEBRUARY

Civilization does not lie in a greater or lesser degree of refinement, but in an awareness shared by a whole people. And this awareness is never refined. It is even quite simple and straightforward. To see civilization as the work of an élite is to identify it with culture, which is something quite different. There is a Mediterranean culture. But there is also a Mediterranean civilization. At the other extreme, one must not confuse the idea of civilization with that of the people.

On Tour (theater)

In the morning, the tenderness and fragility of the Oranais region, so hard and violent under the daytime sun: shimmering watercourses bordered with rose laurel, shades of almost conventional color where the sun is rising, mauve-colored mountains fringed with pink. Everything heralds a glorious day. But with a delicacy and gentleness that one feels will soon be over.

APRIL 1937

Strange: inability to be alone, inability not to be alone. One accepts both. Both profit.

The most dangerous temptation: to be like nothing at all.[2]

Kasbah: there always comes a moment when you draw away from yourself. A small charcoal fire crackling in the middle of a dark and slimy alleyway.

Madness—beautiful setting for a magnificent morning —the sun. The sky and bones. Music. A finger at the window.

The need to be right—the sign of a vulgar mind.

Story—the man who refuses to justify himself.[3] Other people prefer their idea of him. He dies, alone in his awareness of what he really is—Vanity of this consolation.

APRIL

Women—who prefer their ideas to their sensations.

[2] *Ne ressembler à rien.* This idea recurs in the essay on Oran, completed in 1939, and included in *L'Eté* (translated in *The Myth of Sisyphus*, p. 181).

[3] This idea is later developed in *The Stranger*, where Meursault is condemned to death partly because of his refusal to make any attempt to justify himself in the eyes of his judges.

—For the essay on ruins: [4]

The drying wind—the old man stripped as bare as an olive tree in the Western Sahara.

(1) Essay on ruins: the mind among the ruins or death in the sun.

(2) Go back to "Iron in the Soul"—foreboding.

(3) The house before the world.

(4) Novel—work at it.

(5) Essay on Malraux.

(6) Thesis.

In a foreign country, the sun bathing the houses on a hill in golden light. A more intense emotion than that produced by the same sight in one's own country. It is not the same sun. I know perfectly well that it is not the same sun.

In the evening, the gentleness of the world on the bay. There are days when the world lies, days when it tells the truth. It is telling the truth this evening—with what sad and insistent beauty.

MAY

Mistake of a psychology which concentrates on details. Men who are seeking and analyzing themselves. To know oneself, one should assert oneself. Psychology is action, not thinking about oneself. We continue to shape our per-

---

[4] The essay on ruins became *Le vent à Djemila* in *Noces. Iron in the Soul*—title of the essay in *L'Envers et l'Endroit* describing Camus's experiences in Prague, *La Mort dans l'Ame*.

sonality all our life. If we knew ourselves perfectly, we should die.

(1) The wondrous poetry that precedes love.

(2) The man who makes a failure of everything, even his death.

(3) In our youth, we attach ourselves more easily to a landscape than to a man.

It is because landscapes allow themselves to be interpreted.

M A Y

Projected preface for *L'Envers et l'Endroit*.

In their present state, most of these essays will appear rather formless. This does not spring from a convenient disregard for form, but simply from an insufficient maturity. Those readers who take these pages for what they are, that is to say *essays* in the full sense of the word, can be asked only to follow the general development of the ideas they express. They will then perhaps feel, between the first page and the last, a secret movement which gives them unity. I would be tempted to say that this movement justifies their existence, if I did not look upon all attempts at justification as useless, and if I did not know that people always prefer their own idea of what a man is like to what he really is.

To write is to become disinterested. There is a certain renunciation in art. Rewrite—the effort always brings

some profit, whatever this may be. Those who do not suc-
ceed fail because they are lazy.

Luther: "It is a thousand times more important to believe firmly in absolution than to be worthy of it. This
faith makes you worthy, and constitutes true satisfaction."
(Sermon preached at Leipzig in 1519 on *Justification*.)

J U N E

The condemned man visited by the priest every day. Because the neck is sliced off, because the knees give way,
because the body thrusts itself madly toward the earth to
hide itself in a "My God, My God."

And every time, the resistance of the man who doesn't
want this easy way out, and who wants to chew over and
taste all his fear. He dies without a word, his eyes full of
tears.

Philosophies [5] are worth the philosophers who make
them. The greater the man, the truer his philosophy.[6]

[5] Most of Camus's quotations and references from Spengler come
from the *Introduction* to *The Decline of the West*, which he must have
read in M. Tazeront's translation first published in Gallimard's *Bibliothèque des Idées* in 1924. Since he does not always quote accurately
from the French edition, I have taken the liberty of translating the
entries in the *Notebooks* directly into English. Page references in my
notes, however, are to the authorized English translation by Charles
Francis Atkinson, published by Alfred A. Knopf.

[6] Cf. Spengler, p. 41.

The reader is reminded that, for Spengler, civilization is the form
which a culture takes in decline, cf. p. 31: ". . . death following life,
rigidity following expansion."

Civilization versus culture

Imperialism is pure civilization. Cf. Cecil Rhodes—"Expansion is everything"—civilizations are like small islands—a civilization as the inevitable climax of a culture (cf. Spengler).

Culture: the cry of men in the face of their destiny.

Civilization, its decadence: man's desire for wealth. Blindness.

On a political theory about the Mediterranean.

"What I speak about I know."

(1) Economic first principles (Marxism).[7]

(2) Spiritual first principles (The Holy Roman Empire).

The tragic struggle of the suffering world. Pointlessness of the problem of immortality. We are interested in our destiny, admittedly. But *before,* not after.

The consolatory power of Hell.[8]

(1) In the first place, endless suffering has no meaning for us. We imagine moments of respite.

(2) We cannot feel what is meant by the word "eter-

---

[7] The *cahier* itself has the word *Studies* written by the side of this, as an indication that they were subjects which Camus intended to pursue, not expressions of his own views.

[8] The reflections on hell recur, in slightly different form, at the end of *The Myth of Sisyphus,* when Sisyphus is shown as happy in his useless task partly because of the physical sensations which he can still feel (p. 123).

nity." We cannot give any value to it—except in so far as we talk of an "eternal moment."

(3) In Hell, we are still alive with this body—and this is better than annihilation.

Logical rule: singularity has universal value.

Illogical rule: what is tragic is contradictory.

Practical rule: an intelligent man on one plane can be a fool on others.

To be deep through insincerity.

His *little doll,* seen by Marcel. "Her husband was no good at it. One day she said to me: 'It's never like that when he does it.' "

The battle of Charleroi, seen by Marcel.[9]

"Well, they dressed us Zouaves out in extended order. The major said: 'Charge.' And down we went, it was like a ravine with trees in it. They told us to charge. There was no one in front of us. So we went on and on, and kept going. Then suddenly the machine guns started up at us. We all fell down on top of one another. There were so many dead and wounded in the bottom that you could

[9] Marcel's description of the battle of Charleroi was noted down on a loose piece of paper that was later stuck into the *cahier.* Like the other fragments of conversation in the first three *cahiers,* it was written straight out and underwent no corrections in the typescript.

have sailed across the ravine in a boat. Then there were the ones who shouted out: 'Mummy, Mummy.' It was terrible."

"Oh! Marcel, you have got a lot of medals. Where did you win them all?"

"Where? In the war, I tell you."

"What do you mean, in the war?"

"Here, do you want me to bring you the certificates where it's all written down? Do you want me to make you read all about it? What do you think?"

The "certificates" are brought in.

The "certificates" apply to the whole of Marcel's regiment.

Marcel. Well, we're not rich, but we eat well.[1] Look at my grandson now, he eats more than his father. His father needs a pound of bread, he needs two. And you can pile on the sausage and pile on the sardines. Sometimes when he's finished he says: "Yum, Yum," and goes on eating.

JULY

Countryside near *La Madeleine*.[2] Beauty which gives us a taste for poverty. I am so distant from my fever—so little

---

[1] Marcel's remarks about food recur in *L'Envers et l'Endroit,* p. 46, where the Algerian words *soubressade* (a highly flavored red sausage) and *escabèche* (a kind of fish stew) are replaced by *saucisson* and *camembert.*

[2] A district near Algiers.

capable of any pride but that of loving. Keep at a distance. I must express what fills my heart, and express it quickly.

"It doesn't apply." True novel. A man defends a faith all his life. His mother dies. He gives up everything. But the truth of his faith has not really changed. It doesn't apply, that's all.

The flying boat: the glory of metal shining in the bay against the blue sky.

The pine trees, with their yellow pollen and green leaves.

Christianity, like Gide, asks man to hold back his desires.[3] But Gide finds an extra pleasure in doing this, while Christianity looks upon it as a mortification of the flesh. From this point of view, Christianity is more "natural" than Gide, who is an intellectual. But it is not so natural as ordinary people, who quench their thirst at fountains and know that the aim and end of desire is to have enough and more than enough (write "An Apology for Satiety").

Prague.[4] The flight from oneself.
"I would like a room."
"Certainly. For one night?"

---

[3] The reflections on Christianity and Gide recur in *Summer in Algiers*, p. 143 n. of *The Myth of Sisyphus*.
[4] This conversation is repeated in *La Mort Heureuse*. In *L'Envers et l'Endroit*, however, Camus describes how he took the more expensive room and had to economize on food.

"No. I don't know."

"We have rooms at 18, 25, and 30 crowns."

(No reply.)

"Which room would you like, sir?"

"Any one. It doesn't matter." (Looks outside.)

"Porter, take this gentleman's luggage to room number 12."

(He wakes up.)

"How much is that room?"

"30 crowns."

"It's too expensive. I would like a room for 18 crowns."

"Porter, room number 34."

(1) In the train taking him to ". . . ," "X" was looking at his hands.

(2) The man who is still there. But it is a coincidence.

Lyons [5]

Vorarlberg-Halle.

Kufstein—The chapel, and, all along the Inn, the fields under the rain. Loneliness anchoring itself deeply.

Salzburg—Jedermann. St. Peter's Cemetery. The Mirabelle garden and its precious triumph. Rain, phlox—lake and mountains—walk over the plateau.

Linz—The Danube and the working-class suburbs. The doctor.

Budweis—The suburb. Small Gothic cloister. Loneliness.

Budweis—The suburb. Small Gothic cloister. Loneliness.

[5] Travel notes incorporated into *L'Envers et l'Endroit*, in the description of Camus's visit to Czechoslovakia.

Prague—The first four days. Baroque cloister. Jewish cemetery. Baroque churches. Arrival in the restaurant. Hunger. No money. The dead man. Cucumber in vinegar. The one-armed man sitting on his accordion.

*Dresden—*Paintings.

*Bautzen—*Gothic cemetery. Geraniums and sunflowers in the brick arches.

*Breslau—*Drizzle. Churches and factory chimneys. Its own particular kind of tragic feeling.

Plains of Silesia: pitiless and harsh—dunes—Flights of birds from off the sticky ground in the thick morning light.

*Olmütz—*Tender and slow moving plains of Moravia. Sour plum trees and emotions stirred by distant sights.

*Brno—*Poor districts.

*Vienna—*Civilization—protective gardens and an accumulation of luxury. Inward distress hiding away in these silken folds.

Italy

Churches—a particular feeling associated with them: cf. Andrea del Sarto.

Painting: a set and serious world. Confidence, etc.

Note: Italian painting and its decadence.

The intellectual and commitment (fragment).[6]

---

[6] Camus's views on this were expressed in his review of Paul Nizan's *La Conspiration,* in *Alger-Républicain,* November 11, 1938, where he wrote that it was "a problem as trifling as that of immortality, a problem which man settles with himself and on which he must not be judged.

JULY

How unbearable, for women, is the tenderness which a man can give them without love.

For men, how bittersweet this is.

Married couples: the man tries to shine before a third person. Immediately, his wife says: "But you're just the same . . ." and tries to bring him down, to make him share her mediocrity.

In trains: a mother to her child:
"Don't suck your fingers, you dirty thing."
Or: "If you carry on, you'll get such a. . . ."
Id. married couples: the wife gets up in the crowded train.
"Give it to me," she says.
The husband feels in his pocket and gives her the paper she needs.

JULY 1937

For the Gambler's Novel.
Cf. *Les Pléiades:* [7] overflowing cadence. Keep the rules.
Luxurious soul. The adventurer.

Men belong to a political party as they get married. And when we are concerned with a writer, it is by his work that we can best judge the effects of his commitment." He then went on to observe that Montherlant, who "rejects any regimentation," was one of "the most amazing prose writers of his century," while Aragon had declined since joining the Communist Party.

[7] A novel by Gobineau, 1816–1882, which Camus greatly admired.

JULY 1937—Gambler

Revolution, glory, death, and love. What does this mean to me by the side of this something in myself which is so grave and so true?

"And that is?"

"This heavy swelling up of tears," he said, "which is all the taste I have of death."

JULY 1937

The adventurer. Feels clearly that there is nothing further worth doing in art. Nothing great or new is possible—in Western culture, at any rate. Nothing left but action. But anyone with greatness of soul will feel nothing but despair on entering upon this action.

JULY

In the case of voluntary self-denial, one can go without food for six weeks. (Water is sufficient.) When famine deprives us of food, ten days at the most.

Reservoir of real energy.

Breathing habits of the Tibetan yogis. What we should do is apply our methods of scientific study to experiences of this scale. Have "revelations" in which we do not believe. *What I like to do:* remain lucid in ecstasy.

Women in the street.[8] The warm beast of desire that lies curled up in our loins and stretches itself with a fierce gentleness.

AUGUST

On the way to Paris: this fever beating in my temples. The strange and sudden withdrawal from the world and from men. The struggle with one's body. Sitting in the wind, emptied and hollowed out inside, I spent all my time thinking of K. Mansfield, about that long, painful, and tender story of a struggle against illness. What awaits me in the Alps is, together with loneliness and the idea that I shall be there to look after myself, the *awareness* of my illness.

To keep going to the end means not only resisting but also relaxing. I need to be aware of myself, in so far as this is also an awareness of something that goes beyond me as an individual. I sometimes need to write things which I cannot completely control but which therefore prove that what is in me is stronger than I am.

AUGUST

Tenderness and emotion of Paris. The cats, the children, the free and easy attitude of the people. The gray colors, the sky, a great show of stones and water.

[8] The phrase recurs in *La Mort Heureuse*. A number of entries in the *cahiers* tend to confirm the rumors that Camus led a rather vigorous sexual life.

AUGUST 1937 [9]

Every day he went off into the mountains and came back speechless, his hair full of grass, and his body covered with the scratches of a whole day's rambling. And each time it was the same conquest without seduction. He was gradually wearing down the resistance of this hostile country, managing to make himself like the round, white clouds behind the solitary pine tree standing out on the crest of a hill, like the fields of pinkish willow herb, rowan trees, and bellflowers. He was becoming part of this fragrant, rocky world. When he reached the distant summit and saw the immense countryside stretching out before him, he felt not the calm peace of love but a kind of inner pact which he was signing with this alien nature, a truce concluded between two hard and savage faces, the intimacy of enemies rather than the ease of friendship.

Gentleness of Savoy.

AUGUST 1937

A man who had sought life where most people find it (marriage, work, etc.) and who suddenly notices, while reading a fashion catalogue, how foreign he has been to his own life (life as it is seen in fashion catalogues).[1]

[9] A passage written out in pencil.
[1] Camus told Roger Quilliot that this entry reflected his first conscious formulation of the theme of *The Stranger*. These two entries, the second of which sketches out a possible theme for *La Mort Heureuse*,

Part   I—His life until then.

Part II—Life as a game.

Part III—The rejection of compromise and the discovery of truth in nature.

AUGUST 1937

Last chapter? Paris–Marseilles. The descent toward the Mediterranean.

And he went into the water, washing off the dark and contorted images left there by the world. Suddenly, the rhythm of his muscles brought back to life the smell of his own skin. Perhaps never before had he been so aware of the harmony between himself and the world, of the rhythm linking his movements with the daily course of the sun. Now, when the night was overflowing with stars, his gestures stood out against the sky's immense and silent face. By moving his arm, he can sketch out the space between this bright star and its flickering, intermittent neighbor, carrying with him sheaves of stars and trails of clouds. So that the waters of the sky foam with the movement of his arm, while the town lies around him like a cloak of glittering shells.

Two characters. Suicide of one of them?

------

show how the books developed together in Camus's mind. It also shows that, in his first idea of the character at any rate, Camus intended Meursault to be seen as a man who had gone through the experience of the absurd before the story began. For further discussion of this point, cf. my study *Albert Camus, 1913–1960*, pp. 37–8.

AUGUST 1937

The gambler.

"It's going to be difficult, very difficult. But that's no reason for not trying."

"Of course not," said Catherine, raising her eyes to the sun.

The gambler.

Mme X, otherwise a perfect old bag, was a very fine musician.

For novel.

Part I: Traveling theater. Movie. Story of a great love affair (Collège Sainte-Chantal).

AUGUST 1937

Projected plan. Combine life and gambling with life.

Part I—Flight from oneself.

A. Flight from oneself.

B. M. and poverty. (All in the present tense.) Chapters in series A describe the gambler. Those in series B, life until the mother's death (death of Marguerite—different jobs: selling on commission, motorcar spare parts, préfecture, etc.[2]).

Last chapter: Descent toward the sun and death (suicide—death from natural causes).

Part II

[2] The jobs listed here were held by Camus himself. The note "death from natural causes" (*la mort naturelle*) reproduces the title of the first part of *La Mort Heureuse*.

The other way around. A in the present: Rediscovery of joy. House before the world. Liaison with Catherine.

B in the past. Sexual jealousy. Flight.

Part III

All in the present tense. Love and sun. "No," says the waiter.[3]

A U G U S T   1937

Every time I hear a political speech or I read those of our leaders, I am horrified at having, for years, heard nothing which sounded human. It is always the same words telling the same lies. And the fact that men accept this, that the people's anger has not destroyed these hollow clowns, strikes me as proof that men attribute no importance to the way they are governed; that they gamble—yes, gamble—with a whole part of their life and their so-called "vital interests."

What really upsets me is the importance given to reactions of the soul. If you are melancholy, then life with another person becomes impossible. For if you have any nobility of spirit you cannot bear the innumerable questions asked of you. For such feelings can have about as much importance as getting up an appetite or wanting to. . . .

---

[3] The *cahier* manuscript bears the additional remarks: "Woman who commits suicide," thus sketching out the ending of *The Misunderstanding*, which Camus wrote in 1942–1943.

AUGUST 1937

Plan. 3 parts.

PART I

A. In the present
B. In the past

Ch. A1—M. Mersault's day seen from the outside.

Ch. B1—Poor district of Paris. Horsemeat shop. Patrice and his family. The dumb man. The grandmother.

Ch. A2—Conversation and paradoxes. Grenier. Motion pictures.

Ch. B2—Patrice's illness. The doctor. "This extreme twinge of pain. . . ."

Ch. A3—A month on tour with the theater.

Ch. B3—Different jobs (selling on commission, motorcar spare parts, préfecture).

Ch. A4—Story of the great love affair: "You never felt like that again?" "Yes, Madame, with you." Theme of the revolver.

Ch. B4—The mother's death.

Ch. A5—Meeting with Raymonde.

Or alternatively:

I A—Sexual jealousy.
 B—Poor district—the mother.

II A—House before the world—stars.

    B—Overfullness of life.

III Flight—Catherine whom he does not love.

Reduce and condense. Story of sexual jealousy which gives rise to a feeling of exile. Return to life.

"The lesson which he had gone to seek so far off had kept all its value. But only by being brought back to the sunlit country."

Arrival in Prague—up to the moment of departure—illness.

Explanation—Lucile—Flight.

AUGUST

Absence of Spanish philosophers.

Novel: [4] the man who realizes that one needs to be rich in order to live, who devotes himself completely to the acquisition of money, who succeeds, lives and dies *happy*.

SEPTEMBER

This August has been like a gulf—a deep breath before the release of everything in a wild effort. Provence, and something closing up within me. Provence like a woman leaning on my shoulder.

---

[4] This is partly the plot of *La Mort Heureuse,* where Mersault kills for money and dies happy.

Men must live and create. Live to the point of tears—as when standing in front of this house with its round tiles and blue shutters on a cypress-planted hill.

Montherlant: I am the man to whom something happens.

At Marseilles,[5] happiness and sadness—at the very boundaries of myself. Living town that I love. But, at the same time, this bitter taste of loneliness.

SEPTEMBER 8

Marseilles, hotel bedroom. Big yellow flowers on gray wallpaper. Geography of filth. Sticky, muddy corners behind the enormous radiator. Spring mattress, broken light switch. . . . That kind of liberty which comes from dubious and shady places.

M. SEPTEMBER 8

The long road down glistening with sunlight. The dog roses in Monaco and Genoa, cities full of flowers. Blue evenings on the Ligurian coast. My tiredness and longing for tears. This loneliness and thirst for love. Finally Pisa, alive and austere, with its green and yellow palaces, its domes, its elegance along the banks of the severe Arno. All the nobility contained in this refusal to give itself easily to the traveler. A sensitive and demure town. So

---

[5] The description of Marseilles recurs in *La Mort Heureuse*.

close to me at night, in the empty streets, that as I walked there alone my longing to weep at last finds release. The wound that lay open within me begins to heal.

On the walls of Pisa: "Alberto fa l'amore con la mia sorella." [6]

THURSDAY, SEPTEMBER 9

Pisa and its men lying in front of the Duomo. The Campo Santo, with its straight lines and cypress trees at all four corners. One comes to understand the quarrels of the fifteenth and sixteenth centuries—here each town is important, with its own features and profound truth.

There is no other life but that whose loneliness was marked out by the rhythm of my feet along the Arno. No other life but that which quickened my blood in the train going down to Florence. These women's faces, so serious but suddenly dissolving in laughter. One especially, with a long nose and proud mouth, who was laughing. At Pisa, I spent over an hour lounging about on the grass of the Piazza del Duomo. I drank from the fountains, where the water was tepid but so fluid. Going down to Florence, I spent a long time looking at faces, drinking in smiles. Am I happy or unhappy? It's not a very important question. I live with such frenzied intensity.

Things and people are waiting for me, and doubtless I am waiting for them and desiring them with all my

[6] Cf. *Noces*, p. 84. Most of these notes on Camus's visit to Italy in August–September 1937 were used in *Noces*, especially in the essay *Le Désert*.

strength and sadness. But, here, I earn the right to be alive by silence and by secrecy.

The miracle of not having to talk about oneself.

Gozzoli and the Old Testament (in costume).

The Giotto in the Santa Croce. The inner smile of Saint Francis, lover of nature and of life. He justifies those who have a taste for happiness. A soft and delicate light on Florence. The rain is waiting and swelling up the sky. Christ in the tomb by Giottino: Mary clenching her teeth with grief.

Florence. At every church corner, displays of bright, creamy flowers, sprinkled with water and naïve.

Mostra Giottesca [7]

One needs a certain time to realize that the faces in the Italian primitives are those one meets daily in the street. This is because we have lost the habit of seeing what is really important in a face. We no longer look at our contemporaries, and select only what is useful to our aims (in every sense of the word). The Italian primitives do not distort, they "bring to life."

In the Cloister of the Dead, at the Santissima An-

---

[7] The whole of this passage was incorporated in *Noces*, pp. 71–2, and 79–80. Some sentences were added, but few changes were made in the original wording.

nunziata, the sky was gray and full of clouds, the architecture severe, but there is nothing that speaks of death.
There are ledger stones and ex-votos; one man was a loving father and a tender husband, another the best of husbands and a skillful merchant; a young lady, model of
all virtues, spoke French and English "si come il nativo."
(They all created duties for themselves, and today children play leapfrog on the tombs that seek to perpetuate
their virtue.) Here, a young girl was the hope of all her
family: "Ma la gioia é pellegrina sulla terra." But none of
this convinces me. Almost all of them, according to the
inscriptions, had grown resigned, doubtless because they
accepted their other duties. I shall not grow resigned.
With all my silence, I shall protest to the very end. There
is no reason to say: "It had to be." It is my revolt which is
right, and it must follow this joy which is like a pilgrim
on earth, follow it step by step.

The clouds thicken over the cloister and night gradually
darkens the ledger stones bearing the moral virtues attributed to the dead. If someone here told me to write a
book on morality, it would have a hundred pages and
ninety-nine would be blank. On the last page I should
write: "I recognize only one duty, and that is to love." And,
as far as everything else is concerned, I say *no*. I say *no*
with all my strength. The ledger stones tell me that this
is useless, that life is "col sol levante, col sol cadente." But
I cannot see what my revolt loses by being useless, and I
can feel what it gains.

I thought about all this, sitting on the ground with my
back against a column, while the children laughed and
played. A priest smiled at me. Women looked at me with

curiosity. In the church, the organ was playing softly, and the warm color of its harmonies could be heard from time to time through the children's shouts. Death! If I carry on like this, I shall certainly end by dying happy. I shall have eaten up all my hope.

SEPTEMBER

If you say: "I don't understand Christianity, I want to live without consolation," then you are narrow-minded and prejudiced. But if, living without consolation, you say: "I understand and admire the Christian position," you are a shallow dilettante. I am beginning to grow out of being concerned by what people think.

Cloister of San Marco. The sun among the flowers.

Siennese and Florentine primitives. Their insistence on making monuments smaller than men is a result not of an ignorance of the laws of perspective but of a persistence in giving importance to the men and saints whom they depict. Use this in making theatrical décors.

Late roses in the cloister of Santa Maria Novella, and the women on a Sunday morning in Florence. Their uncorseted breasts, their eyes and lips leave you with a beating heart, a dry mouth, and glowing loins.[8]

[8] The phrase about "glowing loins" (*une chaleur aux reins*) was removed before the sentence was incorporated into p. 81 of *Noces*. Cf. also *Noces*, pp. 89–90.

Fiesole

We lead a difficult life, not always managing to fit our actions to the vision we have of the world. (And when I think I have caught a glimpse of the color of my fate, it shoots off out of sight.) We struggle and suffer to reconquer our solitude. But a day comes when the earth has its simple and primitive smile. Then, it is as if the struggles and life within us were rubbed out. Millions of eyes have looked at this landscape, and for me it is like the first smile of the world.[9] It takes me out of myself, in the deepest meaning of the expression. It assures me that nothing matters except my love, and that even this love has no value for me unless it remains innocent and free. It denies me a personality, and deprives my suffering of its echo. The world is beautiful, and this is everything. The great truth which it patiently teaches me is that neither the mind nor even the heart has any importance. And that the stone warmed by the sun or the cypress tree swelling against the empty sky set a boundary to the only world in which "to be right" has any meaning: nature without men. This world reduces me to nothing. It carries me to the very end. Without anger, it denies that I exist. And, agreeing to my defeat, I move toward a wisdom where everything has been already conquered—except that tears come into my eyes, and this great sob of poetry makes me forget the truth of the world.

SEPTEMBER 13

The scent of laurel which you meet at every street corner in Fiesole.

[9] Id., pp. 82–5.

SEPTEMBER 15

In the cloister of San Francesco in Fiesole there is a little courtyard with an arcade along each side, full of red flowers, sun, and yellow and black bees. In one corner, there is a green water sprinkler, and everywhere the humming of bees. A gentle steam seems to rise from the garden as it bakes in the heat. Sitting on the ground, I think about the Franciscans whose cells I have just visited and whose sources of inspiration I can now see. I feel clearly that if they are right then it is in the same way that I am. I know that behind the wall on which I am leaning there is a hill sloping down toward the town, and the offering of the whole of Florence with all its cypress trees. But this splendor of the world seems to justify these men. I put all my pride in a belief that it also justifies me, and all the men of my race, who know that there is an extreme point at which poverty always rejoins the luxury and richness of the world. If they cast everything off, it is for a greater and not for another life. This is the only meaning which I can accept of a term like "stripping oneself bare." "Being naked" always has associations of physical liberty, of harmony between the hand and the flowers it touches, of a loving understanding between the earth and men who have been freed from human things. Ah, I should become a convert to this if it were not already my religion.

Today, I feel free about the past and about what I have lost. All I want is this compactness and enclosed space— this lucid and patient fervor. And like the warm bread that one kneads and presses I simply want to hold my life between my hands, like the men who knew how to enclose their life between these flowers and these columns. The same is true of those long nights spent on trains, where one can talk to oneself, prepare oneself for life, and feel marvelously patient in taking up ideas again, stopping them in their flight, and then once more moving forward. To lick one's life like a stick of barley sugar, to form, sharpen, and finally fall in love with it, in the same way as one searches for the word, the image, the definitive sentence, the word or image which marks a close or a conclusion, from which one can start out again and which will color the way we see the world. I can easily stop now, and finally reach the end of a year of unrestrained and overstrained life. My effort now is to carry this presence of myself to myself through to the very end, to maintain it whatever aspect my life takes on—even at the price of the loneliness which I now know is so difficult to bear. Not to give way—that is the whole secret. Not to surrender, not to betray. All the violent part of my character helps me in this, carrying me to the point where I am rejoined by my love, and by the furious passion for life which gives meaning to my days.

Every time a man (or I myself) gives way to vanity, every time he thinks and lives in order to show off, this is a betrayal. Every time, it has always been the great misfortune of wanting to show off which has lessened me in the presence of the truth. We do not need to reveal ourselves to others, but only to those we love. For then we are no longer revealing ourselves in order to seem but in order to give. There is much more strength in a man who reveals himself only when it is necessary. I have suffered

from being alone, but because I have been able to keep my
secret I have overcome the suffering of loneliness. To go
right to the end implies knowing how to keep one's secret.
And, today, there is no greater joy than to live alone and
unknown. My deepest joy is to write. To accept the world
and to accept pleasure—but only when I am stripped
bare of everything. I should not be worthy to love the bare
and empty beaches if I could not remain naked in the presence of myself. For the first time I can understand the
meaning of the word happiness without any ambiguity. It
is a little different from what men normally mean when
they say: "I am happy."

A certain persistence in despair finally gives birth to
joy. And the same men who, in San Francesco, live by the
side of these red flowers, keep in their cells a skull to nour-
ish their meditations, seeing Florence from their windows and death on the table before them. And if I now
feel that I have come to a turning point in my life, this is
not because of what I have won but because of what I
have lost. Within me, I feel a deep and intense strength
that will enable me to live as I intend. If, today, I feel so
distant from everything, it is because I have strength
only to love and to admire. Life with its face of tears and
sun, life in the salt sea and on warm stones, life as I love
and understand it—as I caress it I feel my love and despair gathering strength within me. Today is not like a
resting place between "yes" and "no." It is both "yes" and
"no." "No," and rebellion against everything which is
not tears and sunlight. "Yes" to my life, whose future
promise I now feel within myself for the first time. A year
of burning intensity which is coming to an end, and Italy.

I am uncertain of the future, but have achieved total liberty toward my past and toward myself. Here lies my poverty, and my sole wealth. It is as if I were beginning the game all over again, neither happier nor unhappier than before. But aware now of where my strength lies, scornful of my own vanities, and filled with that lucid fervor which impells me forward toward my fate.[1]

September 15, 1937

[1] This literally is the end of the first "Jupiter" *cahier* which Camus filled. His handwriting is at first full and rounded, but gradually becomes tighter and more compact. At the beginning, it varies a good deal from one entry to the next. Toward the end of his life, his handwriting became very small, cramped, and rather difficult to read.

NOTEBOOK II

September 1937 – April 1939

S E P T E M B E R 22

La Mort Heureuse

"You see, Claire, it's rather difficult to explain. There's only one question: to know one's own value. But to do this, you have to leave Socrates on one side. To know yourself you must act—and this does not mean that you can then say who you are. 'The Cult of the Self'—don't make me laugh. Which self and which personality? When I look at my life and at the secret color which it has, I feel as if tears were trembling in my heart. I am just as much the lips that I have kissed as the nights spent in the 'House before the World,' just as much the child brought up in poverty as this frenzied ambition and thirst for life which sometimes carry me away. Many people who know me sometimes don't even recognize me. And everywhere I feel like that inhuman image of the world which is my own life."

"Yes," said Claire, "you're playing it both ways."

"Of course. But when I was twenty, I read like everybody else that all the world's a stage and so on. But that's not what I mean. A number of lives, a number of different levels—of course. But when the actor is on stage, then we accept the convention. No, Claire, we know quite well that this is not play acting, there is something which tells us so."

"Why?"

"Because if the actor gave his performance without knowing that he was in a play, then his tears would be real tears and his life a real life. And whenever I think of this pain and joy that rise up in me, I am carried away by the knowledge that the game I am playing is the most serious and exciting there is.

"And I want to be this perfect actor. I don't care about my personality and I'm not interested in cultivating it. I don't want to treat my life as an experiment, but to be what my life makes me. It is I who am the experiment, and it is life that forms and controls me. If I had enough strength and patience, I know how completely impersonal I would become, how far my strength would carry me on the path to active nothingness. What has always held me back is my personal vanity. Today, I can understand that to love, act, and suffer is indeed to be alive, but only in so far as we become transparent and accept our fate as a single reflection of a rainbow of different joys and passions.

"The road, etc. . . .

"But for that you need time, and now I have time."

Claire, who had said nothing for a long time, now looked into Patrice's eyes and said slowly:

"Much suffering lies in wait for those who love you."

Patrice stood up, an almost desperate look on his face, and said violently:

"Their loving me puts me under no obligation to them."

"That's true," said Claire. "I was just stating a fact. (One day, you will be left alone.)"

SEPTEMBER 23. KIERKEGAARD IN PHILOSOPHICAL FRAGMENTS[1]

"Language is right, in the word 'passion,' to insist on the way the soul suffers. Whereas the way people actually

---

[1] The *Philosophical Fragments* were translated by Knud Ferlov and J. J. Gateau in 1937, and published by Gallimard under the title of *Riens Philosophiques*. This passage occurs on p. 118. I have translated it directly from Camus's French. David S. Swenson translates thus (Oxford University Press, 1936, p. 39): "The Danish language correctly calls emotion (Danish *Affekten*, cf. German *Leidenschaft*) *Sindslidelse*. When we use the word *Affekt*, we are likely to think more immediately of the convulsive daring which astounds us and makes us forget that it is a form of passivity. So, for example, pride, defiance, etc."

Camus seems to have been struck by the resemblance between this note by Kierkegaard and the conversational passage which he himself had written on the previous day. This also seems to be the point of the note about the "perfect actor in life," which is not a quotation from the *Fragments*.

The discussion of Kierkegaard in *The Myth of Sisyphus* deals with a different aspect of this thought, the use of the absurd to justify the leap into religious faith (pp. 36–41). For someone interested in seeing how Camus built up the argument of *The Myth of Sisyphus*, the *Notebooks* are disappointing. They contain, for example, no mention of Husserl, Jaspers, or, more surprisingly, Chestov, and it must be assumed that Camus did make other notes which he destroyed or which have not been made available. The later volumes are equally disappointing as far as the elaboration of *The Rebel* is concerned.

65

use the word makes us think more of how we are over-whelmed by its uncontrollable impetuosity, and thereby forget that it is a question of suffering (pride—a challenge)."

Id. The perfect actor (in life) is the man who is "acted upon"—and who knows it—passive passion.

"He woke up covered in sweat, his clothes all rumpled, and wandered around the flat for a moment. Then he lit a cigarette and sat down, his mind a blank, looking at the creases in his crumpled trousers. His mouth was full of the bitter taste of sleep and tobacco. Around him, his soft and flabby day plashed like ooze."

Rama Krishna on trade:
"The truly wise man is he who feels contempt for nothing."

Do not confuse sanctity with idiocy.

SEPTEMBER 23

Solitude, a luxury of the rich.

SEPTEMBER 26

(1) Put fragments of a diary (ending) at the beginning of the novel.

(2) Remain lucid in ecstasy.

Concrete description: Disappearance of friends.

Streetcars (end of services?).

Ideas—leitmotif.

He sank from silence to silence, huddling down into himself. . . . Until he reached the point where lucidity can turn itself upside down. An immense effort: comes back to the world—drops of sweat—thinks of a woman's open legs—Goes to the balcony and pours out the whole of his being into the world of flesh and light. "It's hygienic."

Then takes a shower and does exercises with his chest expander.

A theologico-political treatise.

In George Sorel. Dedicate to the "left-wing humanism" which tries to make us see Helvétius, Diderot, and Holbach as the high-water mark of French literature.

The idea of progress which infects all working-class movements is a *bourgeois* idea developed in the eighteenth century. "Our whole effort must be to prevent *bourgeois* ideas from poisoning the rising class: this is why we can never do enough to break every link between the people and eighteenth-century literature." (*Illusion du Progrès,* pp. 285 and 286.)

SEPTEMBER 30

I always end up by seeing every aspect there is of a person. It's a question of time. There always comes a moment when I feel the break. What is interesting is that this always happens when I feel this person lacking in curiosity about something.

Dialogue.

"And what do you do in life?"

"I count."

"What?"

"I count. I say: one, the sun; two, the sky (ah, how beautiful it is); three, women; four, flowers (ah, how happy I am)."

"You end up by being silly then."

"Good Lord, you think like your morning paper does. I think like the world does. You share the views of the *Echo de Paris*, and I share those of the world. When it's bathed in sunlight, when the sun beats down, I want to love and kiss, to flow into bodies as into patches of light, to bathe myself in flesh and sunlight. When the world is gray, I feel gloomy and full of tenderness. I feel more moral, so able to love that I could even get married. In either case, it doesn't matter."

After his departure:

(1) A fool

(2) Just showing off

(3) A cynic

"Not at all," says the schoolmistress. "He's a spoiled child, you can see that. A rich man's son, who doesn't know what life's like."

(Because it is increasingly agreed that if you find life can be beautiful and simple you can't know what it's like.)

SEPTEMBER 30

It is in order to shine sooner that authors refuse to rewrite. Despicable. Begin again.

OCTOBER 2

"He strode without stopping through the muddy streets under a fine, light rain. He could see no farther than a few steps in front of him. But he was walking quite alone in this little town that was so far from everything, so far away from everything and from himself. No, it couldn't happen again. To cry about a dog, and in front of everyone. He wanted to be happy. He hadn't deserved that."

OCTOBER 4 [2]

"I lived until the last few days with the idea that I had to do something in life, and more exactly that, because I was poor, I had to earn a living, get a job, settle down. I must accept the fact that the roots of this idea, which I still dare not call a prejudice, were very deep, since it lived on in spite of all my irony and 'last words on the subject.' And then, once appointed at Bel-Abbès, as I was faced with all the permanence that being established there implied, everything suddenly melted away. I rejected it, doubtless because I saw security as unimportant compared to my opportunities for real life. The dull, stifling routine of such an existence made me draw back.

---

[2] One of the rare openly autobiographical passages in the *Notebooks.* Camus had been offered a teaching post at the *collège* of Sidi-bel-Abbès. This entry analyzes his reasons for turning it down.

If I had got through the first few days, I should certainly have accepted. But that was the danger. I was afraid, afraid of being lonely and of being permanently fixed. To-day, I don't know whether it was strength or weakness to have rejected this life, to have shut the door of what people call 'a future' in my own face, and to remain instead poor and insecure. But at least I know that if there is a conflict, it is for something worth while. Unless, later on. . . . No. What made me run away was doubtless the fear not so much of settling down but of settling down permanently somewhere ugly.

"Am I now capable of what other people call 'a serious attitude to life'? Am I lazy? I don't think so, and have given myself proof to the contrary. But have we the right to refuse difficulties under the pretext that we don't like them? I think that only people lacking in character go to pieces through laziness. If I lacked character, there would be only one solution left for me."

OCTOBER 10

To be worth something or nothing. To create or not to create. In the first case everything is justified. Everything, without exception. In the second case, everything is completely absurd. The only choice then to be made is of the most aesthetically satisfying form of suicide: marriage, and a forty-hour week, or a revolver.

On the road to La Madeleine. Once again, in the presence of such great natural beauty, the desire to be stripped bare of everything.

OCTOBER 15

Giraudoux [3] (for once): "The innocence of a being lies in its complete suitability to the world in which it lives."
Ex.: the innocence of the wolf.
The innocent is the person who explains nothing.

OCTOBER 17 [4]

In the paths above Blida, night is soft as milk, and gentle with grace and moderation. In the mornings, on the mountain with its short grass ruffled with meadow saffron, its icy streams, the sun and shade, my body accepts and then refuses. The concentrated effort of walking uphill, the air burning my lungs like a red-hot iron or cutting into them like a sharpened razor, the concentration of all my energy in an effort to go beyond myself and conquer the slope, is like a self-knowledge which one gains through the body. The body, a true path to culture, teaches us where our limits lie.

Villages grouped around natural sites, each living its own life. Men dressed in long white garments, making simple, precise gestures that stand out against the permanently blue sky. Narrow paths bordered with Barbary fig trees, olive, carob, and jujube trees. On these paths,

---

[3] Camus did not like Giraudoux very much, and wrote of his work, in *La Lumière*, on May 10, 1940, that his art consisted solely of "replacing the great themes of fatality by acrobatics performed by the intelligence."
[4] Another passage incorporated into *La Mort Heureuse*. So is the following entry, October 18.

you meet men with brown faces and clear eyes, leading donkeys laden with olives. And these men and trees, gestures and mountains, seen side by side, give birth to a feeling of acceptance mingled with joy and sadness. Greece? No, Kabylia. And it is as if suddenly, across the centuries, the whole of Greece had suddenly been set down between the sea and mountains, reborn in its ancient splendor with its laziness and respect for Fate hardly emphasized by the nearness of the East.

OCTOBER 18

In September, the carob trees breathe a scent of love over all Algiers, and it is as if the whole earth were resting after having given itself to the sun, its belly still moist with almond-flavored seed.

On the road to Sidi-Brahim, after the rain, the scent of love falls from the carob trees, heavy and oppressive, weighed down with all its load of water. Then, as the sun sucks up the water and the colors recover their brightness, the scent of love lessens and becomes hardly noticeable. And it is like a mistress who comes out with you into the street after a whole stifling afternoon, and who, as she leans her shoulder against yours, looks at you in the midst of all the street lights and crowd.

Huxley: "After all, it is better to be a good *bourgeois* like the others than a bad bohemian, a false aristocrat, or a second-rate intellectual. . . ."

72

OCTOBER 20[5]

The demand for happiness and the patient quest for it. We need not banish our melancholy, but we must destroy our taste for difficult and fatal things. Be happy with our friends, in harmony with the world, and earn our happiness by following a path which nevertheless leads to death.

"You will tremble before death."

"Yes, but I shall leave nothing unfulfilled in my mission, which is to live." Don't give way to conformity and to office hours. Don't give up. Never give up—always demand more. But stay lucid, even during office hours. As soon as we are alone in its presence, strive after the nakedness into which the world rejects us. But above all, in order to be, never try to seem.

OCTOBER 21

One needs a good deal more energy to travel with very little money than to play at "the hunted traveler."[6] Traveling steerage, arriving tired out and with a feeling of emptiness, going long distances third class, often eating only once a day, counting one's money and being constantly afraid of having an already very difficult journey interrupted by an unexpected accident—all this requires a

[5] Monsieur Quilliot notes that this is a fragment for *La Mort Heureuse.* I did not find it in the copy which I read, but there is a second typescript, and no indication by Camus as to which is the final version, if one ever existed.

[6] *Voyageur traqué* in French. A reference to Henry de Montherlant's two books, *Aux Fontaines du Désir* and *La Petite Infante de Castille,* to which he gave the general title of *Les Voyageurs Traqués* (1926). Montherlant traveled very extensively from 1924 onward.

courage and will power that make it impossible to take sermons about "the need to uproot oneself" very seriously. It is neither amusing nor easy to travel. If you are young and penniless, you need a liking for difficulties and a love for the unknown if you are to transform your dreams of travel into reality. But, after all, this does save you from dilettantism—although I wouldn't go as far as to say that what is lacking in Gide and Montherlant is the fact that they have never traveled on a cheap ticket which compelled them to spend six days in the same town. But I am perfectly certain that, basically, I·can never see things as Gide or Montherlant do—because of the cheap tickets.

OCTOBER 25

Gossip—unbearable and degrading.

NOVEMBER 5

Cemetery of El Kettar. An overcast sky and a heavy sea facing hills covered with white tombstones. The trees and earth damp from the rain. Pigeons among the white ledger stones. One solitary geranium, its leaves both pink and red, and a great silent feeling of loss and sadness that teaches us to know the pure and beautiful face of death.

NOVEMBER 6

The path to La Madeleine. Trees, earth, and sky. How great a distance and yet what secret understanding between my gesture and the first star awaiting us on our return.

74

NOVEMBER 7 [7]

Character. A.M.—an invalid—both legs amputated—paralyzed all down one side.

"They help me when I want to relieve myself. They wash me. I'm practically deaf. But I would never do a thing to cut short a life in which I believe so strongly. I would accept even worse, blindness, deprivation of all my senses, loss of the power of speech and of any contact with the external world—as long as I could feel within me this dark, burning flame which is me and me alive. And I should still give thanks to life for having let me continue to burn with its flame."

NOVEMBER 8 [8]

In the local movie theater, you can buy mint-flavored lozenges with the words: "Will you marry me one day?" "Do you love me?" written on them, together with the replies: "This evening," "A lot," etc. You pass them to the girl next to you, who replies in the same way. Lives become linked together by an exchange of mint lozenges.

NOVEMBER 13

Cvilinsky: [9] "I've always acted out of spite. Now I get along a lot better. Act so as to be happy? If I am to settle down,

---

[7] The passage is actually spoken by Zagreus in *La Mort Heureuse*.

[8] Incorporated into *Summer in Algiers*, p. 147 of *The Myth of Sisyphus*.

[9] As Monsieur Quilliot points out in his notes to the French edition, Cvilinsky was a doctor in Algiers, and a personal friend of Camus. The passage is spoken by Bernard, the doctor, in *La Mort Heureuse*.

why not here, in a country that I like? But it's always dis-appointing to look forward to things emotionally—always. So we should live in the way we find easiest. Do nothing that goes against the grain, even if we shock people. It's a bit cynical—but it's always the way the most beautiful girl in the world looks at things."

Yes, but I'm not sure that it is always disappointing to look forward to things emotionally. It's just unreasonable. In any case, the only experience I'm interested in hap-pens to be one where everything would be as we expected it. *Doing something in order to be happy, and succeed-ing.* What attracts me is the link between the world and myself, this double reflection that enables my heart to intervene and control my happiness up to the exact point where the world can either destroy it or bring it to fruition.

Aedificabo et destruam, says Montherlant. I prefer to say: Aedificabo et destruat. I don't go from one side of my nature to the other, but from the world to myself and from myself back to the world. It's a question of humility.

NOVEMBER 16

He said: "We must have one love, one great love in our life, since it gives us an alibi for all the moments when we are filled with motiveless despair."

NOVEMBER 17

"The Will to Happiness."

Part III. The achievement of happiness.

Several years. Time flows as the seasons change, and that is all.

Part I (Ending). The invalid who tells Mersault: "Money. It's a kind of spiritual snobbery that makes people think they can be happy without money."

Back home, M. looks at the events in his life in the light of these facts. Reply: "Yes."

For a man who is "nobly born," happiness lies in taking on the fate of everyman, not through a desire for renunciation but with a will to happiness. To be happy, you need time. Lots of time. Happiness too is a long patience. And it is the need for money that robs us of time. Time can be bought. Everything can be bought. To be rich means having time to be happy when you deserve happiness.[1]

NOVEMBER 22

It is normal to give away a little of one's life in order not to lose it all. Six or eight hours a day so as not to die of starvation. And then—there is profit in all things for anyone really in search of it.

DECEMBER[2]

The rain as thick as oil on the windows, the empty sound of horses' hooves, and the dull, persistent downpour all assumed bygone features whose heavy gloom soaked into Mersault's heart as the water soaked into his shoes and

---

[1] Zagreus makes similar remarks about the importance of money in *La Mort Heureuse*.

[2] Another passage in *La Mort Heureuse*.

the cold through the thin material of his trousers into his knees. The whole sky was covered with a mass of rolling black clouds, following unceasingly one after the other. The vaporized water that drifted down, neither mist nor rain, was washing Mersault's face with a gentle hand, laying bare the deep rings under his eyes. The crease had gone from his trousers, and with it that warmth and confidence that a normal man carries around in a world which is made for him.

(At Salzburg.[3])

Irony with Marthe—leaves her.

The man who showed all kinds of promise and who is now working in an office. He does nothing apart from this, simply going back home, lying down and smoking until dinner time, going back to bed again and sleeping until the next morning. On Sundays, he gets up very late and stands at the window, watching the sun or the rain, the passers-by or the silent street. The whole year through. He is waiting. He is waiting for death. What good are promises anyway, since in any case. . . .[4]

Politics, and the fate of mankind, are shaped by men without ideals and without greatness. Men who have great-

[3] Presumably Camus either wrote this passage in Salzburg or is describing something that happened to him there.

[4] Applies both to Mersault and to Meursault. The idea that the inevitability of death destroys all values is fundamental to *The Stranger*. Cf. Meursault's closing speech.

ness within them don't go in for politics. The same is true of everything. But our task now is to create a new man within ourselves. We must make our men of action into men of ideals, and our poets into captains of industry. We must learn to live out our dreams—and to transform them into action. Previously, men gave up or lost their way. We must neither lose our way nor give up.

We haven't the time to be ourselves. All we have time for is happiness.

Oswald Spengler: *The Decline of the West.*[5]
(1) Form and reality:
"I call understanding the world being at its level."
"The man who gives definitions [6] has no knowledge of destiny."
"There also exists in life, apart from causal necessity [7]— which I shall call the logic of space—the organic necessity of destiny—the logic of time. . . ."
The Greeks' lack of any sense of history.
"History, from the earliest times up to the Medic Wars, is the product of an essentially mythical mode of thought." [8]
Originally, the Egyptian column was made of stone and

[5] Cf. footnote 5, p. 35, on Spengler.
[6] *Understanding the world—gives definitions.* Cf. Preface, p. xiv.
[7] Cf. Introduction, p. 7, logic of space, logic of time.
[8] Introduction, p. 10. The idea occurs again in *The Rebel*, 1951, where Camus writes (p. 161): "Aristotle, to give a definite example, did not believe that he was living after the Trojan war."
On the West's Vita Nuova, cf. Spengler, p. 14. All these other remarks are taken from the Introduction to *The Decline of the West.*

the Doric column of wood. This was how the Attic soul expressed the deep hostility which it felt toward any idea of permanence. "Egyptian culture, the incarnation of the idea of care." The Greeks, a happy people, have no history.

The myth, and its anti-psychological meaning. In contrast, what we find at the beginning of the spiritual history of the West is a fragment of self-analysis, and that is the West's Vita Nuova. (Cf. in contrast: the mythical fragments about Heracles, which remain the same from Homer to the tragedies of Seneca. A thousand years. That is to say: Antiquity = the present.)

Ex.: "It was the Germans who invented mechanical clocks, these terrifying symbols of the flow of time, whose sonorous chimes ring out by day and night from innumerable towns in Western Europe, and which are perhaps the most gigantic expression that a historical attitude toward the world is capable of producing."

"As men of Western European culture, endowed with a sense of history, we are the exception and not the rule."

Stupidity of the pattern: Classical times—Middle Ages —Modern Times.

"What meaning can the person of the superman have for the world of Islam?"

"The destiny of a culture is to produce a civilization. Thus Rome follows Athens. The Greek *soul* and Roman *intelligence*. In the classical world, culture becomes civilization in the fourth century, in the West in the nineteenth."

Our literature and music are made for city dwellers.

Thus we make the History of Philosophy the only serious theme of every philosophy.

The whole question:
the antithesis between history and nature
Mathematics   History
and paintings (revise).

D E C E M B E R [9]

What we found moving was her way of hanging on to his clothes, of squeezing his arm when walking along with him, the complete trust with which she gave herself and which appealed to the man in him. There was also her silence, which made her coincide exactly with what she happened to be doing, and completed her resemblance to a cat, which was linked with the gravity she put into her kisses. . . .

At night, he ran his fingers over her high and ice-cold cheekbones, and felt them sink into the soft warmth of her lips. Then he felt as if, somewhere within himself, a great, impersonal, and burning cry had been uttered. And as he stood watching both the night, laden to a bursting point with stars, and the town, like an upturned sky, swollen with human lights, the deep warm breath that rose from the port brought him a thirst for that lukewarm stream, a limitless desire to carry off from those living lips the whole meaning of the inhuman and sleeping world, as if it were a silence locked away within her mouth. He bent down, and it was as if he had placed his lips upon a bird. Marthe groaned. He bit into her lips, and, as their mouths clung together for minutes on end, breathed in that gentle warmth which carried him into ecstasy as if he

[9] Another fragment for *La Mort Heureuse*.

were clasping the whole world in his arms. She, in the meantime, clinging to him like a drowning woman, flashed out from time to time from the great depths into which she had been thrown, thrust his lips away and then drew them to her again, falling back into the black and icy waters which burned her like a people of gods.

DECEMBER

A man who is something of an actor is always happy in the company of women. Women are an appreciative audience.

It is always at the beginning that wearisome things weary us. Later on, there comes the numbness of death. "I shall never be able to live like that." But it is the fact that you do live like that which enables you to accept it.

Novel. Part I. Game of cards (brisque).
The conversations.
"When we were in the Zouaves. . . ."
"With my husband. . . ."
A man who's had a drop too much: "You're disgusting. Disgusting. And I'll tell you why. Because you're a narrow-minded little bastard. And I don't like narrow-minded bastards. *You've no idea of how to live.*"
(Parc Saint-Raphael.)
Novel. Titles: A pure heart.
　　　　　　　The happy on earth.
　　　　　　　The golden beam.

"Do you know many men 'in love' who would refuse an attractive woman if she offered herself to them? And if there are any, it's because they don't have the right temperament."

"You call 'having the right temperament' being devoid of any serious emotions?"

"Quite. (At least in the way you mean serious.)"

Novel. Part I.

Zagreus's house in the country, just outside the town. The room is too warm. Mersault, feeling his ears growing redder and redder, can't breathe. He catches cold on going out into the air (origin of the illness which will kill him).

Ch. IV. Conversation with Z., begun on the subject of "impersonality."

"Yes," says Z., "but you can't do that while you're working."

"No, because I'm in a state of rebellion, and that's bad."

". . . Basically," says M., "I'm a dangerous fanatic."

Novel. Part IV. A passive woman.

"The mistake," said M., "lies in thinking that you must choose, that you must do what you want and that there are conditions for happiness. Happiness either is or it isn't. It's the will to happiness which matters, a kind of vast, ever present awareness. Everything else—women, art, worldly triumphs—are just so many pretexts. An empty canvas for us to decorate."

Novel. Part III.

Some time later, Mersault said he was leaving. He was going to travel, and then settle in the outskirts of Algiers. A month later he was back, now certain that travel had nothing to offer him. He saw it as it really is, a happiness for the restless. This was not what Mersault was looking for in his quest for conscious happiness. Besides, he felt ill and knew what he wanted. For the second time, he made ready to leave the House before the sea.

F E B R U A R Y   1938

Here, men are sensitive to destiny. It is what sets them apart.

The pain of not having everything in common and the misfortune of having everything in common.

F E B R U A R Y   1938 [1]

The spirit of revolution lies wholly in man's protest against the human condition. Under the different forms which it assumes, it is, in this respect, the only eternal theme of art and religion. A revolution is always carried out against the Gods—from that of Prometheus onwards. It is a protest which man makes against his destiny, and both tyrants and *bourgeois* puppets are nothing but pretexts.

This spirit can certainly be grasped in its historical manifestations, but one needs all the emotion of a Mal-

[1] As Monsieur Quilliot points out in his notes to the French edition of the *Notebooks*, these ideas already foreshadow the themes of *The Rebel*.

raux not to give way to the desire to prove. It is simpler to discover it in its essence and destiny. From this point of view, a work of art that retraced the conquest of happiness would be a revolutionary one.

Find excess within moderation.

APRIL 1938

What sordid misery there is in the condition of a man who works and in a civilization based on men who work.

But we must hang on and not let go. The natural reaction is always to scatter your talents outside work, to make people admire you the easy way, to create an audience and an excuse for cowardice and play acting (most marriages are organized on this basis). Another inevitable reaction is to try to be clever about it. Besides, the two things fit in very well together, if you let yourself go physically, neglect your body, and let your will power slacken.

The first thing to do is to keep silent—to abolish audiences and learn to be your own judge. To keep a balance between an active concern for the body and an attentive awareness of being alive. To give up all feeling that the world owes you a living and devote yourself to achieving two kinds of freedom: freedom from money, and freedom from your own vanity and cowardice. To have rules and stick to them. Two years is not too long a time to spend thinking about one single point. You must wipe out all earlier stages, and concentrate all your strength first of all on forgetting nothing and then on waiting patiently.

If this price is paid, then there is one chance in ten of escaping from the most sordid and miserable of conditions: that of the man who works.

APRIL

Send off two essays. *Caligula.* No importance. Not mature enough. Publish in Algiers.

Go back to Philosophy and Culture. Leave everything else: Thesis.

Either Biology + *agrégation*

or Indo-China.

Every day, write something in this notebook. In two years' time, write *a work.*

APRIL 1938

Melville leads an adventurous life and ends up in an office. He dies poor and unknown. Loneliness and isolation (the two things are not the same) will finally enable you to exhaust even viciousness and slander. But we must always be ready to forestall viciousness and slander in ourselves.

MAY

Nietzsche.[2] Condemns the Reformation which saves Christianity from the principles of life and love that Cesare

[2] The reference here seems to be to section 61 of *The Antichrist, A Criticism of Christianity* (translation by Anthony M. Ludovici; The Macmillan Co., 1915, pp. 228–9), which reads as follows: "I see a spectacle so rich in meaning and so wonderfully paradoxical to boot, that it would be enough to make all the gods of Olympus rock with immortal laughter,

Borgia was infusing into it. The Borgia Pope was finally justifying Christianity.

What attracts me in an idea is always its piquant and original quality—what is new and superficial in it. I might as well admit it.

C., who plays at seducing people, who gives too much to everybody, but whose feelings never last. Who needs to seduce, to win love and friendship, and who is incapable of both. A fine character to have in a novel, but lamentable as a friend.

Scene: husband, wife, and the gallery.

The husband has some qualities and likes to show off. His wife is very quiet, but ruins all her husband's effects by short, crisp sentences. Thus establishes her own superiority. Her husband controls himself, but the humiliation makes him suffer. This is how hatred is born.

Ex.: With a smile: "Don't try to be more foolish than you are, my dear."

The spectators in the gallery wriggle and smile un

—*Cesar Borgia as Pope* . . . Do you understand me? . . . Very well then, this would have been the triumph which *I* alone am longing for today:—this would have *swept* Christianity *away*. . . . But . . . Luther saw the corruption of the Papacy when the very reverse stared him in the face: the old corruption, *peccatum originale*, Christianity *no* longer sat upon the Papal chair! But Life! The triumph of Life! The great yea to all lofty, beautiful and daring things . . ." As footnote 8, pp. 96–7, points out, there are many parallels between Camus's early ideas and those of Nietzsche, and the interest which Camus shows in other figures of the Italian Renaissance underlines his similarity to Nietzsche.

comfortably. He blushes, goes toward her, and smiles as he kisses her hand: "You're quite right, my dear."

Face is saved and hatred grows fatter.

I can still remember the despair that overwhelmed me when my mother told me that "now I was old enough, and would get useful presents at New Year's." Even today, I can't stop myself from wincing secretly whenever I receive this type of present. And, certainly, I knew that it was the voice of love—but why must love sometimes take on such ridiculous tones?

One thinks differently about the same thing in the morning and in the evening. But where is truth, in the night thought or in the spirit of midday? Two replies, two races of men.

MAY[3]

The old woman who dies in the old people's home. Her friend, the friend she has made over a period of three years, weeps "because she has nothing left." The caretaker of the little mortuary, who is a Parisian and lives at the mortuary with his wife. "Who could have told them that at seventy-four he would end up at an old people's home at Marengo?" His son has a job. They left Paris. The daughter-in-law didn't want them. Scenes. The old man

---

[3] One of the first fragments for *The Stranger* to have a different atmosphere from the passages for *La Mort Heureuse*. The "little old man" becomes Pérez in the final version, where many other details noted down here are also retained.

finally "raised his hand to him." His son put them in an old people's home. The gravedigger who was one of the dead woman's friends. They often went to the village together in the evening. The little old man who insisted on following the procession to the church and then to the cemetery (two kilometers). Since he is an invalid, he cannot keep up and walks twenty yards behind. But he knows the country and takes short cuts that enable him to catch up with the procession several times until he falls behind again.

The Arab nurse who nails down the coffin has a cyst on her nose and wears a permanent bandage.

The dead woman's friends: little old people ridden with fancies. Everything was wonderful in the past. One of them to a neighbor: "Hasn't your daughter written to you?" "No." "She might remember that she does have a mother."

The other has died—as a sign and a warning to them all.

JUNE

For *Mort Heureuse:* A series of letters breaking off an affair. A familiar theme: it's because I love you too much.

And the last letter: a masterpiece of lucidity. But here again, the amount of play acting is immense.

End. Mersault drinks.

"Oh," said Céleste,[4] wiping the counter. "You're getting old, Mersault."

[4] Céleste, one of Camus's own three favorite characters (cf. Brisville, op. cit., p. 258), appears both in *La Mort Heureuse* and *The Stranger* as the owner of the restaurant where Mersault and Meursault eat.

Mersault stopped short and put down his drink. He looked at himself in the glass above the bar. It was true.

Summer in Algiers.

For whom does this sheaf of black birds fly across the green sky? The blind and deaf summer which filters through and gives a purer sound to the cries of the swifts and the newsboys' shouts.

June. For the summer:

(1) Finish Florence and Algiers.
(2) Caligula.
(3) The summer impromptu.[5]
(4) Essay on the theater.
(5) Essay on the forty-hour week.
(6) Rewrite novel.
(7) The absurd.

For *The Summer Impromptu.*
"You there in the audience."
"What?"
"Yes, you."
"What?"
"Not many of you, are there?"
"What do you mean, not many?" (He looks around.)
"Not many, I mean. There aren't many of you. Just a few."

---

[5] The summer impromptu was written for the Théâtre de l'Equipe, which often performed to very small audiences.

"We do what we can."

"Of course. And we like you like that."

Novel.

"I must admit that I have serious faults," said Bernard. "For example, I'm a liar."

"?"

"Oh, I know. There are some faults that people never confess. And others that it costs nothing to acknowledge. With a tone of false humility, of course:. 'It's true, I'm quick-tempered, gluttonous.' In a way, they find it flattering. But being deceitful, vain, or envious are things that people don't admit. It's always the others who are like that. And besides that, by admitting that you are hasty-tempered, you avoid talking about the rest. You're not going to look for extra defects in a man who has just accused himself spontaneously, are you?

"I have no merit. I have accepted myself. It is this which makes everything so simple."

Caligula: "What you will never understand is that I am a simple man."

An essay on the forty-hour week.

In my family: ten hours' work, followed by sleep. From Sunday to Monday—unemployment: the man weeps. His greatest misery is that he should both weep and wish for what humiliates him (competition).

People talk a lot nowadays about the dignity of work, and about the need for it. Monsieur Gignoux,[6] in particular, has very definite ideas on the subject.

But it's a fraud. There is dignity in work only when it is work freely accepted. Only idleness has a moral value because it can serve as a criterion by which to judge men. It is fatal only to the second rate. That is its lesson and its greatness. Work, on the other hand, crushes everyone down to the same level. It provides no basis for judging men. It brings into action a metaphysic of humiliation. Under the form of slavery which the society of right-thinking people now give it, the best men cannot survive its effects. . . .

I suggest that we stand the usual expression on its head and make work a fruit of laziness. There is a "dignity of labor" in the little barrels which men make for themselves on Sundays. Here, work and play come together again, and play linked with technique attains the dignity of a work of art and of creation itself.

Then there are some people who are indignant or go off into raptures. "What, I tell you, some of my workmen earn 40 francs a day."

End of the month, when the mother says with an encouraging smile: "This evening, we'll have *café au lait.* It's a change from time to time." But at least they might make love. . . .

---

[6] Monsieur Quilliot notes that this is probably the well-known contemporary economist. There is a C. J. Gignoux who is at present editor of the conservative *Revue des Deux Mondes.*

The only fraternity which is now possible, which is offered or allowed to us, is the sordid and sticky fraternity in the face of death in battle.

JUNE

In the movies, the little woman from Oran sitting next to her husband, the tears streaming down her face at the misfortune of the hero. Her husband begs her to stop. In the middle of her tears she says: "But let me make the most of it."

La Mort Heureuse:

In the train, Zagreus is sitting in front of him. However, instead of the black scarf he usually wore, he put on a very light colored summer tie. (After the murder, he goes back to living in his flat. Changes nothing in it. Simply puts in a new mirror.)

The temptation shared by all forms of intelligence: cynicism.

The misery and greatness of this world: it offers no truths, but only objects for love.
Absurdity is king, but love saves us from it.

There is sound psychology in serial stories. But it is a generous psychology, which pays no attention to details. It trusts people, and it is there that its falseness lies.

The old woman and her New Year wishes: We don't ask for very much. Work and good health.

The peculiar vanity of man, who wants to believe and who wants other people to believe that he is seeking after truth, when in fact it is love that he is asking this world to give him.

It is difficult to realize that one can be superior to a large number of people without thereby becoming someone superior. And in that lies his genuine superiority.

AUGUST

One room opens out onto the courtyard, its other door leading into a second room whose only light comes from the first, and which then leads to a third, windowless room. Three mattresses in this third room. Three people sleep there. But since, at its widest point, it is narrower than the length of a mattress, the end of each mattress has been bent up against a wall, and the men sleep in an arc.

The blind man who goes out at night between one o'clock and four with another blind friend. Because like that they are sure of not meeting anyone in the street. If they bump into a lamppost, they can laugh in comfort. They do. Whereas by day, other people's pity prevents them from laughing.

"I ought to write," says the blind man. "But no one's interested. What interests people in a book are the signs of a sorrowful existence. And our lives are never like that."

To write, one must always remain just this side of the words (rather than go beyond them). In any case, no gossip.

The "real" experience of loneliness is one of the least literary there is—a thousand miles away from the idea of loneliness that you get from books.

Cf. the degradation involved in all forms of suffering. One must not give in to emptiness. Try to conquer and "fulfill." Time—don't waste it.

The only liberty possible is a liberty as regards death. The really free man is the one who, accepting death as it is, at the same time accepts its consequences—that is to say, the abolition of all life's traditional values. Ivan Karamazov's "Everything is permitted" is the only expression there is of a coherent liberty. And we must follow out all the consequences of his remark.

AUGUST 21, 1938

"Only he who has known 'the present' really knows what hell is like." (Jacob Wassermann.[7])

Lois de Manou:

---

[7] Probably the German novelist (1837–1934). I have not been able to trace either the exact source of this quotation or the reference to Lois de Manou.

"A woman's mouth, a young girl's breast, a child's prayer, and the smoke rising from a sacrifice are always pure."

On conscious death, cf. Nietzsche: *Twilight of the Idols*, p. 203.[8]

Nietzsche: "It is to the most spiritual souls, assuming them to be the most courageous, that it is given to live out the most painful tragedies. But it is for this reason

[8] The reference here is to the standard *Mercure de France* edition of Henri Albert's translation of *The Twilight of the Idols* (14th edition, 1920; in the 1952 edition the passage is on page 163). Ludovici translates as follows: "One should die proudly when it is no longer possible to live proudly. Death should be chosen freely—death at the right time, faced clearly and joyfully and embraced while one is surrounded by one's children or other witnesses. . . . In spite of all cowardly prejudices, it is our duty, in this respect above all to reinstate the proper, that is to say the physiological, aspect of so-called natural *death*, which after all is perfectly 'unnatural' and nothing else than suicide. One never perishes through anybody's fault but one's own. The only thing is that the death which takes place in the most contemptible circumstances, the death that is not free, the death that occurs at the wrong time, is the death of a coward. Out of the very love one bears to life, one should wish death to be different from this—that is to say, free, deliberate, and neither a matter of chance nor of surprise." The direct translation of the French text referred to by Camus runs: ". . . . a wholly different death, a free and conscious one in which there is no surprise." Cf. *The Twilight of the Idols* (The Macmillan Co., 1915, page 89). The section is number 36 in *Skirmishes in a War with the Age* and is entitled *A Moral for Doctors*.

Ludovici translates the next quotation, section 17 of the same chapter, as: "The most intellectual men, provided they are also the most courageous, experience the most excruciating tragedies; but on that very account they honour life, because it confronts them with its most formidable antagonism."

The passage on conscious death seems to have inspired the first part of *La Mort Heureuse*, which is entitled *Mort Naturelle* and tells how Mersault killed Zagreus when the latter was fully prepared for it. There are a number of close parallels between some of Camus's early ideas and the later philosophy of Nietzsche, and Camus continued to quote his aphorisms in essays and interviews in later life. (Cf. *L'Eté*, p. 74; *The Myth of Sisyphus*, pp. 95–6: "Art and nothing but art; we have art in order not to die of life"; Nobel Prize Speech; Brisville, op. cit., p. 261, and many other occasions.) In the period covered by the *Notebooks*, the four qualities

that they honor life, because it is to them that it shows its greatest hostility."

Nietzsche: "What do we desire when we look at beauty? To be beautiful ourselves. We imagine that beauty carries with it great happiness, but this is a mistake." (*Human, too human.*[9])

The air is peopled with cruel and fearsome birds.

To increase the happiness of a man's life is to extend the tragic [1] nature of the witness that he bears. A truly

---

which the two thinkers have in common are an admiration for "heroic" periods like the Italian Renaissance; a hostility to the "life-denying" aspect of Christianity; a determination to face up to the tragic nature of existence and see in this awareness the source of man's greatness; and, finally, an ambition to combine an attentive concern for the body with intellectual lucidity. It may also be that the frequent mention of the idea of scorn and contempt in 1939–1940 also owes something to Nietzsche; it may equally well have been a purely spontaneous reaction on Camus's part, or a reflection of his admiration for Montherlant.

There is a long discussion of Nietzsche in *The Rebel*, pp. 57–71, where at the same time that Camus recognizes Nietzsche's partial responsibility for the rise of national socialism, he also argues that we must not confuse him with Rosenberg, and that we must "be his advocates." "In the whole history of human intelligence," he continues, "with the single exception of Marx, there is no equivalent for the adventure of Nietzsche. We shall never finish repaying the injustice done to him." In so far as one looks upon *The Rebel* as a personal confession, it is the passage on Nietzsche which strikes the most strongly autobiographical note, for many of Camus's criticisms of Nietzsche's nihilism seem equally applicable to his own earlier attitudes.

[9] Aphorism no. 149: "The slow arrow of beauty."

[1] An idea repeated in *Noces*, p. 152: "In this Algerian summer I learn that one thing only is more tragic than suffering, and that is the life of a happy man. But it may be also the way to a greater life because it leads to not cheating."

tragic work of art (if it does bear witness) will be that of a happy man. Because this work of art will be entirely wiped out by death.

Method used in meteorology. The temperature varies from one moment to the next. It is something too fleeting to be established in mathematical concepts. Here, observations are arbitrary slices of reality. And only the idea of an average enables us to offer an image of this reality.

Etruscan bibliography:

A. Grenier: "Recherches Étrusques" in *la Revue des Etudes Anciennes*, IX (1935)—pp. 219 ff.

B. Nogara: *Les Étrusques et Leur Civilisation*—Paris, 1936.

Fr. de Ruyt: *Charon, Démon Étrusque de la Mort.* (Reference?)

Belcourt

The young woman whose husband takes a siesta and must not be disturbed by the children. Two rooms. She puts a blanket on the floor in the dining room and plays silently with the children so that he can sleep. Because of the heat, she keeps the landing door open. Sometimes, she drops off to sleep herself, and as you go by you can see her lying back, her silent children around her watching the slight movements of her body.

Belcourt

Been fired. Don't dare tell her. Talks.

"Well, we'll have coffee tonight. It makes a change from time to time."

He looks at her. He has often read stories about poverty in which the woman is "brave." She hasn't smiled. She has gone back to the kitchen. Brave? No, resigned.

The former boxer who has lost his son. "What do we do on earth? We move around, and move around."

Belcourt [2]

Story of R. "I knew a woman . . . you might say she was my mistress. . . . I realized there was something funny going on." Story of the lottery tickets ("Did you buy one for me?"). Story of the two-piece dress and her sister. Story of the bracelets and the pawn ticket.

Worked out on the basis of 1300 francs. That doesn't give her enough: "Why don't you work half-days? You'd help me a lot for all these little things. I bought you the suit, I give you 20 francs a day, I pay the rent, and you spend the afternoon drinking coffee with your friends. You give them the coffee and sugar. I give you the money. I've been good to you, and you're doing me wrong."

He wants some advice. He still "likes to have it now and

[2] This is a sketch for the first part of *The Stranger*, where Meursault becomes involved with his rather dubious neighbor Raymond Sintès. *The Stranger*, pp. 30–42.

then." He wants a letter with "nasty things in it" and "things to make her feel sorry."

Ex.: "You just want to have a good time with it, that's all." And then: "I'd thought that . . ." etc.

"You don't see that the world's jealous of all the happiness I'm giving you."

"I knocked her around, but nicely, as you might say. She yelled, I closed the shutters."

The same thing with her friend.

He wants it to be she who comes back. There is something tragic about him in this liking to humiliate people. He is going to take her into a hotel and call the vice squad.

Story of his friends and of the beer. "You lot, you say you're in the underworld." "They told me that if I wanted they would carve her up."

Story of the overcoat. Story of the matches.

"One day, you'll realize how happy I made you."

She is an Arab.

Theme: the world of death. A tragic work: a happy work.

"But, Mersault, it doesn't seem as if this world satisfies you, from the way you talk about it."

"It doesn't satisfy me because it's going to be taken from me—or, rather, it's because it satisfies me too much that I can feel all the horror of losing it."

"I don't understand."

"You don't want to."

"Perhaps."

After a while, Patrice goes away.

"But, Patrice, there is love."

He turned back, his face distorted with despair.

"Yes," said Patrice, "but love is of this world." [3]

Old people's home (the old man cutting across the fields). Burial. The sun melts the tar of the roads—people's feet sink down into it and leave the black flesh gaping open. There is something similar between this black mud and the driver's boiled leather hat. And all these shades of black, the sticky black of the open tar, the dull black of the clothes, the shiny black of the hearse—the sun, the smell of leather and horse dirt, of varnish and incense. Tiredness. And the other man, cutting across the fields.[4]

He is going to the burial because she is his only friend. At the home, they used to say: "She's your fiancée," as if he were a child. And he used to laugh. And he was happy.

Characters.

(A) Etienne, "physical" character; the attention he gives to his body:

1° Watermelon.

2° Illness (twinges of pain).

3° Bodily needs—Good—Warm, etc.

---

[3] The juxtaposition of the passages from *The Stranger* with what is obviously a conversation intended to figure in *La Mort Heureuse* emphasizes the difference in style and atmosphere between the two novels, which were developing together in Camus's mind at that time.

[4] The description of the heat at the funeral is taken up again in *The Stranger*.

4° He laughs with pleasure when he eats something he likes.

(B) Marie C. Her brother-in-law, and their life together, "he pays the rent."

(C) Marie Es. Childhood. Her place in the family. Her virginity, discussed by everyone. Saint Francis of Assisi. Suffering and humiliation.

(D) Mme Leca. Cf. above.

(E) Marcel, the chauffeur—and the old woman in the café.

We do not have feelings which change us, but feelings that suggest to us the idea of change. Thus love does not purge us of selfishness, but makes us aware of it and gives us the idea of a distant country where this selfishness will disappear.

Resume work on Plotinus.[5]

Theme: Plotinian reason.

(1) Reason—not an unambiguous concept. Interesting to see how it behaves in history at a time when it must either adapt itself or perish.

Cf. Diplôme.

It is the same reason, and it is not the same.

[5] Camus had completed his thesis on Plotinus in 1936. There is a good summary of it in Carl A. Viggiani's "Camus in 1936: The Beginnings of a Career," in *Symposium*, Spring–Fall 1958, pp. 12–18. This attempt to pursue the question further does not seem to have led to any published work. There is, however, a reference to this idea in *The Myth of Sisyphus*, pp. 47–8.

It is because there are two kinds of reason, the one ethical and the other aesthetic.

Pursue further: images in Plotinus as the syllogism of this aesthetic form of reason.

The image as a parable: the attempt to express the undefinable nature of feeling by what is obvious and undefinable in concrete things.

As in all descriptive sciences (statistical—collecting facts) the great problem in meteorology is the practical one of deciding how to replace missing data. And the methods used always fall back on the concept of an average, and thereby presuppose the generalized and rational quality of an experience whose rational aspect was the very thing originally sought for.

Belcourt. The speculator in sugar who commits suicide in the lavatory.

The German family in 1914. Four months' respite. They come to fetch the father. Concentration camp. Four years without news. Life during this period. He comes back in '19. Tubercular. Dies after a few months.

The little girls at school.

Artist and work of art.[6] The true work of art is the one which says least. There is a certain relationship between

---

[6] These reflections on art are repeated, with relatively few changes, in *The Myth of Sisyphus*, p. 100.

the global experience of an artist, his thought and his life (his system, in one sense—leaving out anything systematic which this word implies), and the work reflecting this experience. This relationship is wrong when the work gives the whole of this experience surrounded by a fringe of literature. It is right when the work of art is a section cut out of his experience, the facet of a diamond in which the gem's inner luster is reflected but not exhausted. In the first case, there is exaggeration, and literature. In the second, a work which is fruitful because of a whole implied content of experience whose wealth is not directly expressed.

The problem is to acquire that knowledge of life (or, rather, to have lived) which goes beyond the mere ability to write. So that, in the last analysis, the great artist is first and foremost a man who has had a great experience of life (it being understood that, in this case, living also implies thinking about life—that living is, in fact, precisely this subtle relationship between a man's experience and his awareness of it).

If to love implies spending one's life loving, and creating a particular kind of life, then pure love is a love which is dead. It becomes nothing more than a point of reference, and we still need to seek an understanding about all the rest.

Thought is always out in front. It sees too far, farther than the body, which lives in the present.

To abolish hope is to bring thought back to the body. And the body is doomed to perish.

Lying down, he smiled clumsily and his eyes glistened. She felt all her love flood into her throat and tears come into her eyes. She threw herself on his lips and crushed her tears between their two faces. She wept into his mouth, while he tasted in these salt lips all the bitterness of their love.

The dry heart of the creator.

"If only I could read. But in the evening there isn't enough light for me to knit. So I have to lie down and wait. It's a long time, two hours spent like that. Ah, if my granddaughter were here I could talk to her. But I'm too old. Maybe I smell. My granddaughter never comes. So I stay like this, all alone."

2 P.[7]

Today, mother died. Or it might have been yesterday, I don't know. I had a telegram from the home: "Mother died. Funeral tomorrow. Yours faithfully." It doesn't mean anything. It might have been yesterday.

[7] What subsequently became the opening sentences of *The Stranger* were written straight out without any corrections. The note "2P" (second part?) gives the impression, when taken in combination with the plans on pp. 46–50, that Camus may originally have intended to describe the kind of person Meursault was before his discovery of the absurd and his mother's death.

As the concierge said: "It's hot in the plain. You bury them more quickly, especially here." He told me he came from Paris and had found it hard to get used to things. Because, in Paris, you can stay with the body for two, sometimes three days. Here, you don't have the time. You've just got used to the idea that they're dead when you have to start running after the hearse.

. . . But the procession was going too fast as well. And the sun was beating down like a great bully. And as the assistant nurse very rightly said: "If you go too slowly, you risk getting sunstroke. And if you go too fast, you're covered in perspiration and then you catch a chill in the church." She was right. There was no way out.

The undertaker's assistant said something to me that I didn't quite catch. He was lifting his hat up from time to time and using his handkerchief to wipe his head. "What?" I said to him. "Hot," he replied, pointing to the sky. "Yes," I said. "That your mother?" "Yes." "Was she old?" "So-so," I replied, since I didn't know exactly. Then he fell silent.

DECEMBER 1938

For *Caligula:* There is nothing worse than anachronism in the theater. This is why Caligula doesn't say the only reasonable thing that he might say: "A single person thinks, and all is emptiness."[8]

---

[8] Caligula's anachronism is, in French, an ironic misquotation of Lamartine's famous line: "Un seul être vous manque et tout est dé-peuplé." In the original *cahier*, Camus had in fact written out the whole of this line in full, but then crossed out "vous manque" and replaced it with "qui pense."

Caligula. "I need people to keep silent around me. I need living beings to be silent so that the fearful turmoil in my heart can also come to an end."

DECEMBER 15

The prison ship.[9] Cf. description in newspaper.

At the meeting.[1] The old railwayman, clean, well shaven, his shoes shining, his plaid-lined overcoat carefully folded inside out and carried over one arm, who asks me "if it's here" that the meeting is going to take place, and tells me how worried he is when he thinks about what the working man is going to be like in the future.

At the hospital. The tubercular patient who is told by the doctor that he has five days to live. He anticipates and cuts his throat with a razor. Obviously, he can't wait five days.

One of the male nurses tells the journalists: "Don't mention it in your papers. He's suffered enough already."

The man who loves *on this earth* and the woman who loves him with the certainty of finding him again in the hereafter. Their loves are not on the same scale.

[9] A reference to Camus's article in *Alger-Républicain*, December 1, 1938.

[1] Perhaps a reference to his article on November 27, 1938. (See list of Camus's articles in Appendix A.)

Death and a writer's work. Just before dying, he has his last work read over to him. He still hasn't said what he had to say. He orders it to be burned. And he dies with nothing to console him—and with something snapping in his heart like a broken chord.

SUNDAY

The wind in the mountain holding us back, gagging us, shouting in our ears. The whole forest twisted from top to bottom. Above the valleys, the red ferns flying from one mountain to the next. And this beautiful orange-colored bird.

Story of the foreign legionary who kills his mistress in the back room of a café. Then he takes the body by the hair, drags it into the main room, and then out into the street, where he is arrested. He had invested some money in the café, and the owner had told him not to bring his mistress there. She had come all the same. He ordered her to leave. She refused. That was why he killed her.

The little couple in the train. Both ugly. She hangs on to him, laughs, flirts, tries to seduce him. He looks gloomy, is embarrassed that everyone can see him being loved by a woman he is not proud of.

High society, or the two old journalists exchanging insults in the middle of the police station, surrounded by a circle of grinning policemen. Senile fury, unable to express itself in blows, comes out in an astonishing excess of filth: "Filthy bastard—old whore—stupid cunt—little pimp."

"Me, I'm a respectable man."

"That's the big difference between us."

"Yes, a big difference. I'm respectable. You're just a stinking son of a bitch."

"Shut up or I'll knock you silly and kick the shit out of you."

"You're about as strong as my bow tie. Because I'm respectable, you see."

Spain. The man who is a party member. He wants to enlist. After the interview, it turns out that it is for personal reasons. *Rejected.*

In every life, there are a great number of small emotions and a small number of great emotions. If you make a choice: two lives and two types of literature.

But, *in fact,* they are two monsters.

The pleasure that one takes in male relationships. The subtle pleasure of giving or asking for a light—a complicity, a kind of freemasonry of the cigarette.

P. who says he is prepared to offer "a miniature of the Virgin, pregnant, in a frame of toreador's collarbones."

Notice in the barracks: "Drink drives out the man and brings out the beast." Which makes men understand why they like it.

"The earth would be a magnificent cage for animals totally lacking in humanity."

It is to Jeanne [2] that some of my purest joys are linked. She often used to say to me: "You're silly." It was her expression, the one she used when she laughed, but she always said it when she loved me most. We both came from poor families. She lived a few streets away from me, in the *rue du centre*. Neither of us ever went out of our own neighborhood, for everything brought us back to it. And in both our homes we found the same sadness and the same sordid life. Our meetings were a way of escaping from all this. Yet today, when I look back over so many years and see her face, like a tired child's, I realize

[2] The first fragment in the *Notebooks* to be later used in *The Plague*. Roger Quilliot, who has had access to the different manuscripts for his preparation of the *Pléiade* edition, notes that in the first version of the novel this fragment was written by the sentimental classics master, Stephan. A note to this effect in the French edition of the *Notebooks* led a reviewer in the *Times Literary Supplement* for July 6, 1962 (p. 487) to suggest that the passage might perhaps refer to Camus's first wife. M. Quilliot assures me that this is a complete misreading of his note. In any case, Simone Hie, Camus's first wife, was the daughter of a doctor, whereas Jeanne remains a railroad man's daughter in the final version of this episode in *The Plague*, where she is the wife of the clerk, Grand. Cf. *The Plague*, pp. 74–5.

that we were not really escaping from it, and that what is now priceless in our love stemmed from the very shadow which this poverty cast over us.

I think that I really did suffer when I lost her, but I had no feelings of rebellion. This is because I have never really felt at ease in ownership. Regret has always seemed much more natural to me. And although I can see my feelings quite clearly, I have never been able to stop thinking that Jeanne is much more a part of me at a moment like today than she was when she stood a little on tiptoe to put her arms around my neck. I can't remember how I met her. But I know that I used to go to visit her at her home. Her father worked on the railroad, and when he was at home he always sat in a corner, looking thoughtfully out of the window, his enormous hands flat on his thighs. Her mother was always doing housework. So was Jeanne, but in such a light and carefree manner that she never looked as if she was really working. She wasn't very small, but always looked so to me. And I felt she was so light and tiny that I always had a twinge of sadness when I saw her dart across the road in front of the trucks. I can see now that she was probably not very intelligent. But at the time, I never thought about it. She had her own particular way of playing at being cross that almost made me cry with delight. And this heart, now closed to so much, can still be touched by the memory of the secret gesture she would make when she turned around and threw herself into my arms when I begged her to forgive me. I can't remember now whether I wanted her physically or not. I know that everything was mixed up, and that all my feelings melted into tenderness. If I did want her, I forgot about it the first day that, in the corridor of her flat, she kissed me to thank me for a little brooch that I had given her. With her hair drawn back, her uneven mouth with its rather large teeth, her clear eyes and straight nose, she looked that evening like a child that I had brought into the world for the sake of its love and tenderness. Helped by Jeanne herself, who always called me her "big friend," I kept that impression for a long time.

There was a strange quality to the joys we shared together. When we got engaged, she was eighteen and I twenty-one. But what filled our hearts with grave and joyful love was the official character that it now had. And for Jeanne to come home with me, for mother to kiss her and call her "my girl," were all opportunities for rather ridiculous moments of joy that we made no attempts to hide. But Jeanne's memory is linked in my mind with an impression that I shall never be able to express. I can still feel it, however, and I only need to be sad, see a woman whose face touches me, and then come across a brilliantly lit shop front, to find Jeanne with me again, her face turned toward me as she says: "How lovely," and be hurt by the truth of the memory. It was at Christmas time, and the local shops made a great show with lights and decorations. We would stop in front of the confectioners' windows. The chocolate models, the imitation rockwork of gold and silver paper, the snowflakes of cotton wool, the gilded plates and rainbow-colored cakes, all sent us into raptures. I felt a little ashamed. But I could not hold back the upsurge of joy that filled my whole being and brought tears to Jeanne's eyes.

If, today, I try to analyze this feeling, I can find many

different things in it. Certainly, this joy came first and foremost from Jeanne—from her scent and the way she used to hold tightly on to my wrist, or pout her lips. But there was also the sudden brightness of the shops in a neighborhood that was normally so dark, the hurried air of the passers-by, laden with parcels, the delight of the children in the streets, which all helped to tear us from our world of loneliness. The silver paper around the chocolates was the sign that a confused but noisy and golden period was beginning for the simple-hearted, and Jeanne and I snuggled closer together. Perhaps we were vaguely aware of the particular happiness that a man feels when his life falls into harmony with what he is himself. Normally, we carried the magic desert of our love through a world from which love had disappeared. And on days like these, it seemed that the flame which rose in us when we held hands was the same one which we saw dancing in the shop windows, in the hearts of the workmen who had turned around to look at their children, and in the depths of the pure and icy December sky.

D E C E M B E R

Faust the other way around. The young man asks the devil for the goods of this world. The devil (who wears a sports coat and likes to say that cynicism is the great temptation of intelligence) gently replies: "But you already have the goods of this world. You must ask God for what you lack— if you really do think that you do lack anything. You can strike a bargain with God, and in exchange for the goods of the next world you can sell him your body."

After a pause, the devil lights an English cigarette and says: "And that will be your eternal punishment."

Peter Wolf. Escapes from a concentration camp, kills a sentry, and reaches the frontier. Seeks refuge in Prague, where he tries to start his life again. After the Munich agreement, is extradited by the Prague govern-' ment. Handed over to the Nazis. Condemned to death. Executed with an ax a few hours later.

On a door: "Come in. I have hanged myself." [3] They go in and find it is true. (He says "I," but there isn't an "I" any more.)

Javanese dances. Slowness the basis of Hindu dances. The spreading out of the limbs. The detailed efflorescences in the group movements. Like the accumulation of details in architecture. Nothing is hurried, everything takes its course. It is neither an action nor a gesture, but a participation.

By the side of this, tragedy expressed by the leaps in certain cruel dances. The use of silences by the accompaniment (which, moreover, is like a musical ghost). Here, the music does not describe the pattern followed by the dance. It forms a background. It enfolds the gestures

[3] M. Quilliot points out that, in the first version, it is Stephan, the narrator, who hangs himself. In the final version, it is Cottard, who later becomes a black-marketeer.

and the music. It flows around the bodies and their imperceptible geometry.

(*Othello* in the dance of the heads.)

For the end of *Noces*.

The earth! Man's task is to fill this great temple deserted by the gods with idols made in his own image, indescribable, with faces of love and feet of clay.

. . . these monstrous idols of joy, with a face of love and feet of clay.

The deputy for Constantine who is elected for the third time. At noon on election day he dies. In the evening, people go to his house to cheer him. His wife goes out on the balcony and tells them that her husband is a little tired. Shortly afterwards, the corpse is elected deputy. Most appropriate.[4]

On the Absurd? [5]

There is only one case in which despair is pure: that of the man sentenced to death. (May I be allowed a short illustration?) A man driven to despair by love might be

[4] The comment on the death of the deputy for Constantine parallels the account which Camus gave of a senatorial election in Algiers in *Alger-Républicain* on October 24, 1938, when he wrote: "201 senatorial delegates have conferred on Monsieur Mallarmé the right to frustrate, by his presence in the Senate, the hopes and desires of a whole department."

[5] First draft of an idea which links together *The Myth of Sisyphus* and *The Stranger*. The character of Kirilov, from Dostoevsky's *The Possessed* (which Camus adapted for the stage in 1959), is studied on pp. 104–12 of *The Myth of Sisyphus*.

asked if he wanted to be guillotined on the following day and would refuse. Because of the horror of the punishment? Yes. But here, the horror springs from the complete certainty of what is going to happen—or rather, from the mathematical element which creates this certainty. Here, the Absurd is perfectly clear. It is the opposite of irrationality. It is the plain and simple truth. What is and would be irrational is the fleeting hope, itself already near to death, that it is all going to stop and that this death can be avoided. But this is not what is absurd. The truth of the matter is that they are going to chop his head off while he knows what is happening—at the very moment when his whole mind is concentrated on the fact that his head is going to be chopped off.

Kirilov is right. To commit suicide is to prove that one is free. And there is a simple solution to the problem of liberty. Men have the illusion that they are free. But when they are sentenced to death they lose the illusion. The whole problem lies in whether or not it is real in the first place.

Before: [6] "This heart, this little sound that has been with me for so long, how can I imagine that it will ever cease beating, how can I imagine this at the very moment when. . . ."

"Oh, prison, prison, the paradise of prison."

(The mother: "And now they are giving him back to me. . . . This is what they have done with him. . . . They have given him back to me in two pieces.")

"Eventually, I slept only a little during the day, and

[6] A first draft of Meursault's reflections when awaiting execution. *The Stranger,* pp. 142–3.

waited at night for dawn to break, bringing with it the truth of another day. For the whole of that uncertain hour when I knew that *they* usually came. . . . Then I became like an animal. . . . Afterwards, I had another day.

"I worked it out. I tried to control myself. There was my appeal. I always assumed the worst. It was rejected. Well then, I would die. Perhaps sooner than others. But how often had not the idea of dying made me see life as absurd? Since we are going to die anyway, it doesn't matter how and when. Therefore I must accept. Then, at that moment, *I had the right* to consider the other possibility. I was pardoned. I tried to tame the upsurge in my body and blood which made my eyes smart with desperate hope. I tried to make this cry less intense, so as to make my resignation more plausible if my first assumption were correct. But what was the use. The dawns came, and with them the uncertain hour. . . .

"But here they are. Yet it's still very dark. They've come earlier. I've been robbed, I tell you I've been robbed. . . .

"Run away. Wreck everything. No, I'll stay. Cigarette? Why not. Time. But at the same time, he's cutting my shirt collar away. At the same time. I haven't gained any time at all. I tell you I'm being robbed.

". . . How long this corridor is, but how quickly these people are walking. . . . As long as there are a lot of them, as long as they greet me with cries of hatred. As long as there are a lot of them, and I am not alone. . . .

". . . I'm cold. How cold it is. Why have they left me in my shirt-sleeves? It's true that it doesn't matter any more. No more illnesses for me. I've lost the paradise of suffering,

I'm losing it, as I'm losing the joy of spitting out my lungs, of being eaten away by a cancer under the gaze of someone I love.

". . . And this starless sky, these black windows, and this man in the front row, and the foot of this man who. . . ."

END

The Absurd. Gurvitch.[7] Essay on Despair. Power of the leaders. . . .

Mersault.

Caligula.

Special number of *Rivages* [8] on the theater.

Find the productions again. Commentary on Miquel's [9]

[7] A French sociologist, author of *Les tendances actuelles de la philosophie allemande* and *Les essais de sociologie*.

[8] *Rivages* was the title of a literary magazine which the publisher Charlot—who first published *L'Envers et l'Endroit* and *Noces*—brought out in Algiers. It was called a *Revue de la Culture mediterranéenne*, and Camus wrote an introduction for the first number in 1939. Only two numbers appeared, the second of which published the essay *Summer in Algiers* from *Noces* (one of the essays included in the 1955 translation of *The Myth of Sisyphus*). The special number on the theater does not seem to have been published, but the following manifesto of the Théâtre de l'Equipe appeared in the first number of *Rivages:* "The theater is an art of the flesh which gives living bodies the task of translating its lessons, an art which is both coarse and subtle, demanding an exceptional degree of understanding between movements, voices, and bodies." The Théâtre would put on, continued the advertisement, works from civilizations where "the love of living mingled with the despair of life." Examples of these were Greece, Elizabethan England, Spain, and modern America.

[9] Louis Miquel was an Algerian architect and a friend of Camus. M. Quilliot notes that he was responsible, with Simounet, for making the plans of the Centre Albert Camus, a sportsground opened at Orléansville in 1960.

plan. Presentation. Everything concerned with the theater.

The Mirabel garden in Salzburg.

The company on tour at Bordj-bou-Arreridj.

1939

To burn is rest for me. Other things burn apart from joy. But unending work, unending marriage, or unending desire.

Order of work:

Lecture on the theater.

Read about the absurd.

Caligula.

Mersault.

Theater.

Rivages at Charlot's on Monday.

Lesson.

Paper.

FEBRUARY

Lives which death does not take by surprise. Which have organized themselves for it. Which have taken it into account.

In the same way as a writer's death makes us exaggerate the importance of his work, a person's death makes us exaggerate the importance of his place among us. Thus the past is wholly made up of death, which peoples it with illusions.

A love which cannot bear to be faced with reality is not a real love. But then, it is the privilege of noble hearts not to be able to love.

Novel. These conversations side by side, at night, these endless shared and spoken secrets.

"And this life of waiting. I wait for dinner and then for sleep. I think about waking up the next morning, with a vague hope—but of what? I don't know. I wake up and wait for lunch. And so on until the next day. . . . Always to be saying to myself: "Now he's at his office, he's having lunch, he's at his office, he's finished work—and this gap in his life which I have to imagine, that I do imagine and that makes me cry out with pain. . . ."

". . . Arrive joyfully to set out the next day—and how close despair is to joy! Looking back to these two days. They were wonderful, and tears cover them over."

Algeria, country of both excess and moderation. Measured in its lines, excessive in its heat.

Death of "Caporal." Cf. newspaper.

The lunatic in the bookshop. Cf. newspaper.

Tragedy forms a closed world, in which we stumble over and knock against obstacles. In the theater, tragedy must be born and die in the restricted area of the stage.

Cf. John Stuart Mill: "Better to be a dissatisfied Socrates than a satisfied pig."

This morning full of sunlight. The streets warm and full of women. Flowers on sale at every street corner. And the smiling faces of these young girls.

MARCH [1]

"Once in this warm, well-lit, first-class compartment, I closed the door behind me and lowered all the blinds. Then, sitting in the midst of the extraordinary silence which suddenly greeted me, I felt as if a great weight had suddenly been lifted away. I was freed from all the breathless days that I had just lived through, from the effort to bring my life under control, from a whole turmoil of difficulties. Everything was silent. The coach was vibrating gently. And although I could still hear the sound of the rain brushing across the windows, it seemed to form part of the silence. For the next few days I no longer had to think, but merely to travel. I had become a prisoner of

---

[1] Another passage for *La Mort Heureuse*, the last one that Camus seems to have written. (Cf. notes to Introduction.) He here seems to be experimenting with the possibility of making Mersault tell his story in the first person. It will be noted, however, how different the style is from that of Meursault in *The Stranger*.

timetables, hotels, of a human task that was waiting for me. Now that I had ceased to belong to myself, I had achieved true self-possession. And I closed my eyes in ecstasy over the calm which accompanied the peaceful universe, freed from tyranny and love, that had just come to birth outside myself."

Oran. Mers-el-Kébir bay above the little garden of red geraniums and freesias. A day of sunshine and clouds, not of unbroken fine weather. A country in harmony with itself. A long break in the clouds is enough to bring calm flooding back into overanxious hearts.

APRIL 1939

In Oran, a "sufoco" is an insult. You don't stand for it, but pay it back at once, in blood. The Oranais are hot-blooded.

A landscape can be magnificent without being great. It can even narrowly miss greatness. The bay of Algiers, for example, misses greatness because it is too beautiful, Mers-el-Kébir seen from Santa Cruz, on the other hand, shows us what beauty is like: magnificent and heartless.

A few yards from the immediate outskirts of Oran, you find unending stretches of uncultivated land, covered at this season of the year with full-flowering broom. A little farther on lies the first village set up by official colonization. It is quite without soul, and in its one solitary street there stands a symbolic bandstand.

The high plateaus and the Djebel Nador.

Unending stretches of cornfields, empty of both trees and men. At long intervals, you see a hut, and a chilly silhouette standing out against the horizon as it crosses a ridge. A few crows, and silence. Nowhere to seek refuge, nothing on which to hang a feeling of delight, or a possibly fruitful melancholy. What rises up from this earth is anguish and sterility.

At Tiaret,[2] some schoolteachers told me they were "damned fed up."

"And what do you do when you're fed up?"

"Get tight."

"And then?"

"Go to the brothel."

I went with them to the brothel. It was snowing. A fine, penetrating snow. They had all been drinking. A doorman made me pay two francs to go in. It was an enormous, rectangular room, painted in an odd pattern of oblique black and yellow bands. People were dancing to a phonograph. The girls were neither pretty nor ugly.

One of them said: "Coming up?"

The man said no, rather half-heartedly.

"Well," said the girl, "I wouldn't mind it at all."

---

[2] Camus went to Tiaret, a town in the southeast of the department of Oran, in order to cover the trial and acquittal of Michel Hodent in March 1939. (Cf. Appendix A).

When we came out, it was still snowing. Through an opening, you could see the countryside. Still the same desolate expanse, except that this time it was white.

At Trezel—a Moorish café. Mint tea and conversations. The street where the prostitutes are is called "Rue de la Vérité." It's three francs a time.

Tolba [3] and his brawls.

"I'm not a bad guy, but I'm very touchy. I hop from right to left. The other guy says to me: 'If you're a man, get off the streetcar.' I say to him: 'Go on, keep your shirt on.' So he says: 'You're not a man.' So I get off and say to him: 'Now then, that's enough, or I'll rough you up.' 'You and who else?' So I give him one. Down he goes. I go to help him up. And he tries to kick me. So I shove my knee in his face and slap him a couple of times. There's blood all over his face. So I say: 'Had enough?' 'Yes,' he says."

Mobilization [4]

The eldest son is leaving. He's sitting in front of his mother and saying: "It won't come to anything." The

[3] This story is repeated, by Raymond Sintès, in *The Stranger*, pp. 35–6. Camus took a great interest in the local speech habits of people in Algiers, and seems to have had a knack for remembering all the details of conversations that he overheard. It is impossible for a translation to give anything like the impression of the original French.

[4] Perhaps a personal reminiscence of Camus's elder brother Lucien going off to war in 1939.

mother says nothing. She has picked up a paper that was lying on the table. She folds it into two, then into four, then into eight.

At the station, the crowd seeing people off. Men packed into the carriages. A woman crying. "But I never thought it would be like this, that it would hurt so much." Another: "It's funny, people rushing off like that to get killed." A girl cries in her fiancé's arms. He looks grave and says nothing. Smoke, shouts, and jolts. The train leaves.

Women's faces, delights of the sun and sea—that is what is being murdered. And if one doesn't accept murder, then one has to hang on. We're living right in the middle of a contradiction, the whole of our century is stifling and living up to its neck in this contradiction, without a single tear to relieve its anguish.

Not only is there no solution, but there aren't even any problems.

NOTEBOOK III

April 1939 – February 1942

Whereas in Provence or in Italy cypress trees are usually dark patches against the sky, here, in the El Kettar cemetery, this cypress tree was streaming with light, overflowing with the golden wealth of the sun. It seemed as if a golden juice had come boiling up from its black heart to the utmost tips of its short branches, and were flowing in long wild trails along the green leaves.

. . . Like those books where too many passages are underlined in pencil to make people think highly of the previous reader's taste and judgment.

Dialogue between Europe and Islam: [1]

"And when we look at your cemeteries and what you have made of them, we feel a kind of pitying admiration for you, a horror mingled with esteem for men who have to live with such an image of their death. . . .

". . . We too often feel self-pity. It helps us to live. It is a feeling that you hardly know, and you would find it unmanly. Nevertheless, it is felt by those among us who are highest in many virtues. For we call manly those who are wholly lucid, and reject any strength which is divorced from complete awareness. For you, on the other hand, a man's virtue lies in giving orders."

At war. People who argue about the amount of danger at each front. "Mine was the most dangerous." When everything has been made vile and sordid, they still try to establish an order of merit. That is how they survive.

"Yes," said the sewerman, "and you ought to see the lavatories that 'they've' made for them down there at the naval barracks. It's a real shame to give lavatories to people like that."

The woman who lives with her husband without understanding a thing about him. One day, he talks on the radio. They put her behind a pane of glass where she can

[1] The dialogue between Europe and Islam has a number of affinities with Malraux's *Temptation of the West* (1926).

see but not hear him. All she can see is that he is making certain gestures. For the first time, she sees him in his body, as a physical being, and also for the clown he is.[2]

She leaves him. "It's that puppet who climbs onto my belly every night."

Subject for a play. The masked man.

After a long journey, he comes back home wearing a mask. He keeps it on for the whole play. Why? That's what the play is about.

At the end, he takes it off. There was no reason for it. It was just to see things from behind a mask. He would have been ready to keep it on a long time. He was happy, if there is any meaning to that word. But what makes him take it off is the way his wife suffers. He says to her:

"Up to now, I loved you with my whole being, and now I shall love you only as you want to be loved. It seems that you prefer to be despised rather than to love without knowing why. There are two kinds of greatness here."

(Or two women. One loves him with his mask because he fascinates her. Then, she stops loving him. "You loved me with your mind. You had to love me with your body as well." The other loves him *in spite of* the mask, and continues afterwards.)

By a strange but natural reaction, she imagined that it was the things which hurt her most that caused suffering to the man she loved. She had so accustomed herself to

[2] The idea of realizing how absurd somebody is by watching him through a pane of glass recurs in *The Myth of Sisyphus*, p. 15.

M. Quilliot notes that the "masked man" is the first sketch for *The Misunderstanding* (1944).

doing without hope that as soon as she tried to understand this man's life, she always saw only what was un-
favorable to herself. And that was exactly what annoyed
him.

The historical and the eternal mind. One has a feeling
for beauty. The other for infinity.

Le Corbusier: "What makes an artist, you see, are the
moments when he feels that he is more than a man."

Pia [3] and the documents that will disappear. A deliberate crumbling away. Faced with nothingness, the reaction of hedonism and constant travel. Here, the historical
mind becomes geographical.

In the streetcar. The man who is half drunk and at-
taches himself on to me. "If you're a man, give me five
francs. Look, I've just come out of the hospital. Where
am I going to sleep tonight? But if you're a man, I'll go and
have a drink and I'll forget. I'm unhappy, I am. I haven't
got anyone."

I give him five francs. He takes my hand, looks at me,
throws himself into my arms, and bursts out sobbing. "Ah,
you're a good guy. You understand me. I've got no one,
you understand, no one." When I have left him, the

[3] Pascal Pia was the editor of *Alger-Républicain* in 1938–1939, and later
worked with Camus on *Combat*. *The Myth of Sisyphus* is dedicated to him.

streetcar starts up again and he stays inside, lost and still in tears.

The man who has lived alone for a long time and who adopts a child. He pours out onto him his whole lonely past. And in the tight little universe in which he lives, constantly with the child, he feels himself master, and the ruler over a magnificent kingdom. He bullies and frightens the child, drives him mad with his whims and violent demands. Until, one day, the child runs away and the man finds himself alone again, with his tears and a terrible upsurge of love for the toy that he has just lost.

"I would wait for the moment when, out in the street, she used to look up at me. And what I then saw was a pale and shining countenance, which had been cleansed of make-up and made almost expressionless by my kisses. Her features were bare. And for the first time, it was really her that I was seeing, after having sought her during all the long, stifling hours of desire. The patience with which I had loved her at last had its reward. And it was in this face, with its paler lips and white cheekbones, which my mouth had exhumed from its shell of smiles and make-up, that I finally reached her and knew her deeply."

Poe and the four conditions for happiness.
(1) Life in the open air.
(2) The love of another being.

(3) Freedom from all ambition.
(4) Creation.

Baudelaire: "They forgot two rights in the Declaration of the Rights of Man. The right to contradict oneself, and the right to leave."
Id. "There are some temptations which are so strong that they must be virtues."

Madame du Barry, on the scaffold: "Just a moment, executioner."

July 14, 1939. A year ago.

On the beach: a man, his arms in the form of a cross, crucified in the sunlight.

With Pierre, obscenity is like a form of despair.

"These terrible years of doubt when he waited for marriage, or for anything at all—during which he was already building up the philosophy of renunciation which would justify his failure and cowardice."

"With his wife. The problem was to discover whether a man such as he could live among this woman's lies without forfeiting his own integrity."

AUGUST

(1) Oedipus puts an end to the Sphinx, and casts out mystery by his knowledge of man. The whole universe of the Greeks is clear.

(2) But it is the same man who is savagely destroyed by destiny, by the implacable destiny of blind logic. The unshadowed light of tragic and mortal things.

See Epicurus (essay).

The grotto of Aglauros on the Acropolis. Minerva's statue, stripped bare of its clothes once a year. Probable that all statues were similarly clothed. Naked Greek statues are our invention.

At Athens, there was a temple consecrated to old age. Children were taken to visit it.

Coresos and Callirhoë [4] (Play).

He sacrifices himself first. On learning of this proof of love, she strikes herself dead.

[4] It is difficult to discover exactly which mythological characters Camus had in mind. According to M. Quilliot's note, Callirhoë was a daughter of a king of Calydon and was loved by Coresos, a priest of Dionysius. She rejected him, and in revenge the priest made the god he served strike all the inhabitants of Calydon with madness. The oracle ordered the sacrifice of Callirhoë, but Coresos preferred to kill himself. Touched by this devotion, Callirhoë killed herself too.

Legend of the gods preaching charity disguised as beggars. Charity was not natural.

At Sicyon, Prometheus tricked Zeus. Two bags made of bull's hide, one containing the flesh, the other the bones. Zeus chose the bones. This is why the use of fire was taken away from mankind. Low vengeance.

The daughter of the potter Dibutades loved a young man and traced the outline of his shadow on a wall. Her father, seeing her sketch, discovered the style of ornamentation used on Greek vases. Love is at the beginning of all things.

At Corinth, two temples stood side by side: those of violence and of necessity.

Dimetos had a guilty love for his niece, who hanged herself. One day, the little waves carried on to the fine sand of the beach the body of a marvelously beautiful young woman. Seeing her, Dimetos fell on his knees, stricken with love. But he was forced to watch the decay of this magnificent body, and went mad. This was his niece's vengeance, and the symbol of a condition we must try to define.

At Pallantion, in Arcadia, there was an altar dedicated to "the pure gods."

I'm ready to die for her, said P. But don't let her ask me to live.

SEPTEMBER 1939. WAR

The people who rush to be operated on by a well-known Algiers surgeon because they are afraid that he will be drafted.

Gaston: "The main thing is that before being drafted, I have time for a good lay."

On the station platform, a mother to a young, thirty-year-old reservist: "Now be careful."

In the streetcar: "Poland's not going to stand for it."

"The 'anti-Comertin pact,' it's as dead as a doornail."

"If you give Hitler your little finger, the next thing you'll be doing is taking your trousers down."

At the market: "We'll have a reply Saturday, you know."
"What reply?"
"Hitler's."
"So what?"
"Well, then we'll know whether it's war."
"Terrible, isn't it?"

At the station, there were reservists slapping ticket collectors on the face and calling them "draft-dodgers."

The war has broken out.[5] But where is it? Where does this absurd event show itself, except in the news bulletins

[5] This passage, M. Quilliot notes, was initially intended for *The Plague.* Later, however, Camus decided not to use it.

we have to believe and the notices we have to read? It's not in the blue sky over the blue sea, in the chirring of the grasshoppers, in the cypress trees on the hills. It isn't in the way the light leaps youthfully in the streets of Algiers.

We want to believe in it. We look for its face, and it hides itself away. The world alone is king, with the magnificent countenance it shows us.

We have lived hating this beast. Now it stands before us and we can't recognize it. So few things have changed. Later on, certainly, there will be mud and blood and an immense feeling of nausea. But today we find that the beginning of a war is like the first days of peace: neither the world nor our hearts know they are there.

. . . Remember the first days of what will probably be a highly disastrous war as days of immense happiness —a strange and instructive destiny. . . . I am seeking reasons for my revolt which nothing has so far justified. . . .

We always exaggerate the importance of an individual life.[6] So many people don't know what to do with theirs that it is not completely immoral to take it from them. On the other hand, everything takes on a new value. But this has already been said. The essential absurdity of this

---

[6] One of the passages which show Camus developing some of the ideas used both in *The Myth of Sisyphus*—universality of the feeling of the absurd—and in *The Plague*—impossibility of standing aside from calamities.

catastrophe does not alter the fact that it exists. It generalizes the rather more essential absurdity of life itself. It makes it more immediate and more relevant. If this war can have an effect on man, it will be to confirm the idea which he has of his own existence and the way he judges it. As soon as this war "is," any judgment which can take it into account is false. A reflective man generally spends his time adapting his idea of things to the alterations imposed by new facts. It is in this process of bending and adjusting thought, in this conscious elimination of error, that truth—that is to say, what life can teach us—is to be found. This is why, however vile this war may be, no one can stand aside from it. I myself first of all, naturally, since I can have no fear in risking my life by wagering on death. And then all the nameless and resigned who go off to this unpardonable slaughter—and who, I feel, are all with me as brothers.

A cold wind comes in through the window.[7]
Mother: "The weather's starting to change."
"Yes."
"Will they keep the electricity low all through the war?"
"Probably."
"It's going to be a gloomy winter, then."
"Yes."

They have all betrayed us, those who preached resistance and those who talked of peace. There they are, all

[7] Perhaps a conversation which Camus had with his mother. It recurs in *The Plague*, p. 112.

as docile and guilty as one another. And never before has the individual stood so alone before the lie-making machine. He can still feel contempt and use it as a weapon. And if he has no right to stand on one side and feel scorn, he still has the right to judge. Humanity in general, the crowd, can offer nothing. It was treason to believe the opposite. We die alone. They are all going to die alone. Let the man who is alone at least keep his scorn, and the ability to pick out from this terrible ordeal what serves his own greatness.

Accept the ordeal and everything which it entails. But swear, in the least noble of tasks, to perform only the noblest of actions. And real nobility (that of the heart) is based on scorn, courage, and profound indifference.

To be born to create, to love, to win at games is to be born to live in time of peace. But war teaches us to lose everything and become what we were not. It all becomes a question of style.

I dreamed that we entered Rome as triumphant conquerors. And I thought of the entry of the Barbarians into the Eternal City. But I was in the ranks of the Barbarians.

Reconcile the descriptive with the explanatory work. Give description its true meaning. When it stands alone, it it admirable but carries no conviction. All we then need to do is make it clear that our limitations have been chosen deliberately. They then disappear, and the work can "prolong its echoes."

"On the one hand," the man said when he had been classed unfit but called in again for another medical check, "it's a damned nuisance. But, on the other, I heard too many jokes. 'Not gone yet?' 'Still around?' There are forty-four men in our building, and I was the only one left. So I came home at night and went out early in the morning."

The other reservist, whose stomach has been X-rayed:
"They made me drink about six pints of chalk. Before, I shat black. Now, I shit white. That's war."

SEPTEMBER 7

We used to wonder where war lived, what it was that made it so vile. And now we realize that we know where it lives, that it is inside ourselves. For most people, it's the embarrassment, the need to make a choice, the choice which makes them go but feel remorse for not having been brave enough to stay at home, or which makes them stay at home but regret that they can't share the way the others are going to die.

It's there, that's where it really is, and we were looking for it in the blue sky and the world's indifference. It is in this terrible loneliness both of the combatants and of the noncombatants, in this humiliated despair that we all feel, in the baseness that we feel growing in our faces as the days go by. The reign of beasts has begun.

The hatred and violence that you can already feel rising up in people. Nothing pure left in them. Nothing unique. They think together. You meet only beasts, bestial European faces. The world makes us feel sick, like this universal wave of cowardice, this mockery of courage, this parody of greatness, and this withering away of honor.

It is terrifying to see how easily, in certain people, all dignity collapses. Yet when you think about it, this is quite normal since they only maintain this dignity by constantly striving against their own nature.

There is one fatality which is death, and outside this all other fatality disappears. In the space of time between birth and death, nothing its predetermined. You can change everything, you can stop the war and even maintain peace, if you want to do so intensely and for a long time.

Rule: Start by looking for what is valid in every man.

Cf. Groethuysen, on Dilthey: [8] "Thus, having recognized the fragmentary nature of our existence, and the accidental and limited quality which one life has when taken

---

[8] Wilhelm Dilthey (1833–1911) was a German philosopher who insisted upon the importance of historical study in the human sciences. He is dealt with in Raymond Aron's *Essai sur la théorie de l'histoire dans l'allemagne contemporaine*, 1939, which was reviewed by Bernard Groethuysen in Vol. CCCXIII of the *Nouvelle Revue Française* for 1939, pp. 622–9. This quotation, however, is not taken from this review, and may be Camus's summary of Groethuysen's argument.

by itself, we shall begin to seek for what we can no longer find within ourselves in a number of lives taken together."

If it is true that the absurd has been fulfilled (or, rather, revealed), then it follows that no experience has any value in itself, and that all our actions are equally instructive. The will is nothing. Acceptance everything. On one condition: that, faced with the humblest or the most heart-rending experience, man should always be "present"; and that he should endure this experience without flinching, with complete lucidity.

It is always useless to try to cut oneself off, even from other people's cruelty and stupidity. You can't say: "I don't know about it." There is nothing less excusable than war, and the appeal to national hatreds. But once war has come, it is both cowardly and useless to try to stand on one side under the pretext that one is not responsible. Ivory towers are down. Indulgence is forbidden—for oneself as well as for other people.

It is both impossible and immoral to judge an event from outside. One keeps the right to hold this absurd misfortune in contempt only by remaining inside it.

One individual's reaction has no intrinsic importance. It can be of some use, but it can justify nothing. The dilettante's dream of being free to hover above his time is the most ridiculous form of liberty. This is why I must try to serve. And, if they don't want me, I must also accept the position of the "despised civilian." In both cases, I am absolutely free to judge things and to feel as disgusted with them as I like. In both cases, I am in the midst of the war, and have the right to judge it. To judge it, and to act.

Accept. And, for example, see the good side of things. If they don't want me to fight, it is because my fate is always to stay on one side. And it is from this struggle to remain an ordinary man in exceptional circumstances that I have always drawn my greatest strength and my greatest usefulness.

Goethe (to Eckermann): "If I had wanted to throw off all forms of constraint, it would have been in my power to cause my own complete ruin and that of everyone around me."

The first thing is to learn to rule over oneself.

On Goethe: "He is tolerant without being indulgent."

A Prometheus—as a revolutionary ideal.

"What does not cause my death increases my strength." (Nietzsche.) [9]

"The desire for a system is a failure in loyalty." (*Twilight of the Idols.*) [1]

---

[9] Cf. *Twilight of the Idols*, tr. Ludovici, maxim 8: *From the military school of life.*

[1] Idem, maxim 26: "The will to a system shows a lack of honesty."

"The tragic artist is not a pessimist. He says 'Yes' to everything terrible and problematical." (*Twilight of the Idols.*) [2]

What is war? Nothing. It matters not the slightest whether one is a soldier or a civilian, whether one joins it or fights against it.

Man as seen by Nietzsche (*Twilight of the Idols*).

"Goethe [3] conceived the idea of a man who would be strong, highly cultured, skillful in all things physical, keeping himself well under control, respecting his own individuality, able to run the risk of fully enjoying all the wealth and range of physical things, and strong enough for liberty; he would be tolerant, not through weakness but through strength, because he knows how to draw profit from what would be the ruin of weaker natures; a man for whom there is now nothing forbidden, except weakness, whether this is called vice or virtue. . . . Such a mind, freed of everything, stands forth in the center of the world, accepting fate with happiness and

[2] Page 23: "The tragic artist is no pessimist—he says *Yea* to everything questionable and terrible, he is Dionysian."

[3] Page 110. My own translation of Camus's French version.

Ludovici's translation reads: "Goethe conceived a strong, highly-cultured man, skillful in all bodily accomplishments, able to keep himself in check, having a feeling of reverence for himself, and so constituted as to be able to risk the full enjoyment of naturalness in all its rich profusion and be strong enough for this freedom; a man of tolerance, not out of weakness but out of strength, because he knows how to turn to his profit that which would ruin the mediocre nature; a man unto whom nothing is any longer forbidden, unless it be weakness either as a vice or as a virtue. Such a spirit, *become free*, appears in the middle of the universe with a feeling of cheerful and confident fatalism; he believes that only individual things are bad, and that as a whole the universe justifies and affirms itself. *He no longer denies. . . .*"

confidence, with the belief that the only things to be condemned are those which exist in isolation, and that, seen
as a whole, all problems resolve themselves in self-affirma-
tion. *He no longer says 'No'. . . ."*

Overcome this as well? I must. But this unceasing effort
is not devoid of sadness. Could this at least have been
spared us? But this weariness must be overcome as well.
Nothing of it will be lost. One evening, when we look in the
mirror, we see a deeper line around our mouth. What is
it? The stuff from which I made the happiness I overcame.

The story of Jarry [4] on his deathbed, asked what he
wanted and replying: "A toothpick." They gave him one,
he put it into his mouth, and died happy. And the misery
and desolation is that people laugh, and no one sees the
terrible lesson. Nothing more than a toothpick, nothing
else but a toothpick, as much as a toothpick—herein lies
the whole value of this inspiring life.

"But this little boy is very ill," said the lieutenant. "We
can't take him." "I'm twenty-six, I have my life, and know
what I want." [5]

After so many others have said the same thing, Paulhan
writes in the NRF to say how amazed he is that the war of

[4] Camus later changed his mind about the author of *Ubu-Roi,* and wrote
of him, in a footnote to *L'Homme Révolté,* p. 119: "Jarry, one of the mas-
ters of Dadaism, is the last incarnation of the metaphysical dandy, but
had more peculiarities than genius."

[5] Presumably an account of Camus's own medical examination, in
which he was rejected as unfit for the army.

1939 should not have begun in the same atmosphere as that of 1914. The simpletons who thought that horror always had the same face, who cannot escape from the physical images on which they have lived.

Spring in Paris; a promise, or a chestnut bud, is enough to make your heart grow tender. In Algiers, the transition is more brusque. It's not a single rosebud but a thousand rosebuds that, one morning, stifle you with their perfume. And we are not moved by the subtle quality of an emotion, but overwhelmed by an enormous flood of a thousand different individual scents and dazzling colors. It is not our subtler feeling which grows more perceptive, but our whole body which has to withstand an atttack.

NOVEMBER 1939

What one uses in war.

(1) What everyone knows about.

(2) The despair of those who don't want to fight.

(3) The pride of those whom nothing compelled to leave but who left in order to avoid being alone.

(4) The hunger of the men who enlist because they have lost their job.

(5) Many noble feelings like:
    (a) solidarity in suffering.
    (b) contempt that wants to remain silent.
    (c) the absence of hatred.

It is all put to a despicable use and it all leads to death.

Death of Louis XVI. He asks the man taking him to the guillotine to deliver a letter to his wife. Reply: "I am not here to run your errands, but to take you to the guillotine."

In Italian museums, you see little painted screens that the priest used to hold before the prisoner's face to hide the scaffold from him.

The existential leap is one of the little screens.[6]

Letter to a man in despair.[7]

You write that you are overwhelmed by the war, that you would agree to die, but that what you cannot bear is this universal stupidity, this bloodthirsty cowardice, and

---

[6] This is repeated in *The Myth of Sisyphus,* p. 91, where it is linked with the idea of remaining aware of the inevitability of death and of the absurdity of life. Thinkers who take the existentialist "leap into faith" are forfeiting this awareness.

[7] This letter to a man in despair is similar in style to but very different in tone and content from the *Letters to a German Friend,* written in 1943–1944. (Cf. *Resistance, Rebellion, and Death.*) The ideas which it puts forth have a number of parallels in the articles which Camus wrote for *Alger-Républicain* and *Soir-Républicain* in 1938–1940. On April 25, 1939, for example, he wrote, in an account of a lecture by M. R. E. Charlier, that "the Versailles Treaty is the spiritual father of the Munich agreements," and, in an unsigned editorial in *Soir-Républicain* for November 6, 1939, that "we think, in fact, that there is only one fatality in history, and it is the one we put there ourselves. We believe that this conflict could have been avoided, and that it could still be ended to everybody's satisfaction." Similarly, on December 18, 1939, Camus wrote of his "conviction that war was not inevitable, since it would have been avoided with better luck." This should not, however, be seen as a sign of Communist sympathies on Camus's part: he wrote in *Soir-Républicain* on December 19, 1939: "The U.S.S.R. is, today, one of the nations of prey. Revolutionary imperialism is still imperialism." Nevertheless, he was still fairly optimistic about the possibility of an early end to the war when he wrote, in the same article, that "a reconciliation of imperialisms can bring about their disarmament."

this criminal simplemindedness which still believes that human problems can be solved by the shedding of blood.

I read and understand you. And what I understand most clearly is the contrast which you make between your own readiness to die and your revulsion at the idea of other people's death. This proves a man's quality, and classes him as someone you can talk to. How, in fact, can we avoid falling into despair? Those we love have often been in danger before, from illness, death or madness, but we ourselves and the things we believe in have still lived on. Often, the values on which our life is built have almost collapsed. But never before have these values and those we love been threatened all together and all at the same time. Never before have we been so completely handed over to destruction.

I can understand you, but I cease to agree when you try to base your life on this despair, maintain that everything is equally pointless, and withdraw behind your disgust. For despair is a feeling, and not a permanent condition. You cannot stay on in despair. And feelings must give way to a clear view of things.

You say: "Besides, what is to be done? And what can I do?" But the question doesn't start by presenting itself like that. You still believe in the individual, since you can feel what is worthwhile both in those around you and in you yourself. But these individuals can do nothing, and so you despair of society. But remember: you and I had already rejected this society a long time before the catastrophe took place; we knew that it was destined to end in war, we both denounced this state of affairs, and both felt that there was nothing in common between this so-

149

ciety and ourselves. It is the same society today, and it has reached its normal end. And, when you look at things dispassionately, you have no more reasons to despair now than you had in 1928. In fact, you have exactly as many, no more and no less.

And, when you really think about it, the men who went off to war in 1914 had more reasons to despair, since they understood things less clearly than we do. You may say that knowing there were as many reasons to despair back in 1928 as they are now, in 1939, doesn't get us any further. This is only apparently true. For you didn't despair completely in 1928, whereas today you find everything completely pointless. If circumstances are the same, then it must be your opinion of them which is wrong. This happens every time that, instead of seeing a truth as reason presents it to us, we see it in the flesh. You had foreseen the war, but thought you could prevent it. And this kept you from falling completely into despair. Today, you think you can no longer prevent anything at all. That is the crux of the argument.

But, first of all, you must ask yourself if you really did do everything necessary to prevent this war. If you did, then you could look on it as inevitable, and you could consider that there is nothing more to be done. But I am not convinced that you yourself, any more than any one of us, did do all you should have done. You couldn't prevent it? No, that is not true. It would have been enough if the Treaty of Versailles had been revised in time. This was not done, and that is all there is to it. You see that things could have happened differently. But there is still time to revise this treaty, or any other cause. We can still make it

unnecessary for Hitler to stick to his word. There is still
time to reject those acts of injustice that have led to other,
similar acts, and thereby make these unnecessary as well.
There is still something useful to be done. You assume
that the role you can play as an individual is practically
nonexistent. But I will reverse my earlier argument and
tell you that it is neither greater nor smaller than it was in
1928. Besides, I know that you are not very set on this
idea of uselessness. For you do not, to my knowledge, support conscientious objection. And this is not because you
lack courage or admiration, but because you don't think
that it does any good. Thus, you already have some notion
of what is useful and what is not which enables you to
follow what I am saying.

There is something for you to do, have no doubt about
it. Every man has at his disposal a certain zone of influence, which he owes as much to his defects as to his
qualities. But whichever is the case, this zone is there,
and can be immediately used. Push no one to rebel. We
must be sparing of other people's blood and liberty. But
you can convince ten, twenty, or thirty men that this war
is not and was not inevitable, that there are ways of pre-
venting it that have not yet been tried, and that we must
say this, writing it when we can and shouting it if we
must. These ten or thirty men will, in turn, tell it to ten
others, who will repeat what the first have said. If laziness
prevents them, so much the worse, start again with others. And when you have done what you can in your own
zone, in your own field, then you can call a halt and despair as much as you like. Understand this: we can despair of the meaning of life in general, but not of the par-

ticular forms that it takes; we can despair of existence, for we have no power over it, but not of history, where the individual can do everything. It is individuals who are killing us today. Why should not individuals manage to give the world peace? We must simply begin without thinking of such grandiose aims. You must realize that men make war as much with the enthusiasm of those who want it as with the despair of those who reject it with all their soul.

A remark quoted by Green in his *Journal*:
"We must not fear death. This would be paying it too much honor."

Green and his *Journal*.
Notes down a number of dreams. I always find this kind of thing boring.

Death of Flaubert's friend, Le Poittevin:
"Close the window. It's too beautiful."

Bordeaux Cathedral. In the corner:
"Great Saint Paul, let me be in the first ten."
"Great Saint Paul, let him come to meet me."

Montherlant, who quotes at the beginning of *Service Inutile* a superb remark by Cardinal Darbout: "Your mistake lies in believing that man was put on this earth to do something." And Montherlant draws from this some magnificent and bitter lessons in heroism. But one could draw exactly the opposite lesson from these words, and justify Diogenes or Ernest Renan. Only great thoughts are capable of such contradictory fruitfulness.

Always struck by the "comical" aspect of everything in Algeria connected with death. I find nothing more justified. Impossible to exaggerate the ridiculous quality of an event that is normally accompanied by sweat and gurgling. Similarly, it could not be too far demoted from the sacred status normally attributed to it. Nothing is more despicable than respect based on fear. And, from this point of view, death is no more worthy of respect than Nero or the inspector at my local police station.

Lawrence: [8] "Tragedy ought to be like a great kick at misfortune." (Cf. his aristocratic communism.)

[8] Both these quotations are from D. H. Lawrence's *Letters*. The first, to A. W. McLeod, was written on October 6, 1912, and the full quotation is: ". . . I hate Bennett's resignation. Tragedy ought really to be a great kick at misery." (*Letters of D. H. Lawrence*, ed. Aldous Huxley, 1932.)

The second is an adaptation of a sentence in Lawrence's letter of December 28, 1928, to Charles Wilson: ". . . It's time there was an *enormous* revolution—not to install soviets, but to give life a chance."

The question of the possible influence of D. H. Lawrence on Camus was discussed by Rayner Heppenstall as early as 1948 in an article in *Penguin New Writing* entitled *Albert Camus and the Romantic Protest*, and taken up by the same critic in *The Fourfold Tradition* in 1960. It is not possible to say whether Camus read Lawrence in French or in English, but the *Letters* were translated by Thérèse Aubray and published by Plon in 1934. Both these letters were included in the translation (Vol. I, p. 33,

Id.: "We should not bring about the Revolution to give power to a class, but to give a chance to life."

M. [9] "Men are not my fellows. They are the people who look at me and judge me. My fellows are those who love me without looking at me, who love me in spite of everything, in spite of failure, betrayal, or humiliation, who love me and not what I have done or shall do, who would love me for as long as I loved myself—up to and including suicide."

. . . "with her alone (his wife May) I have this love in common, whether in anguish or not, as some people share sick children who might die."

---

and Vol. II, p. 224), but there are slight differences between Camus's wording in the *Notebooks* and that of the French translation. I have translated them back into English as they stand, and it will be noticed that the second one, in particular, is not a word-for-word quotation.

Mme Camus told me in August 1962 that her husband, like many of his friends in Algeria, was a great admirer of Lawrence, most of whose novels had been translated into French before the war—*Lady Chatterley's Lover*, it may be noted, with a preface by André Malraux. Camus refers to Lawrence, in a preface to Louis Guilloux's *La Maison du Peuple* (Grasset, 1953), and also quotes the phrase about tragedy in an essay entitled *Les Amandiers*, written in 1940 and reprinted in *L'Eté*, 1954, p. 73. In the typescript of *La Mort Heureuse* there is also a phrase about the "dieux noirs" which Mersault intended henceforth to serve. The reviewer in the *Times Literary Supplement* of July 6, 1962, p. 487, also mentioned a likeness between *Sea and Sardinia* and some of Camus's early essays, and it is certain that there are close similarities of attitude between the two writers.

I should like to thank the readers of the *Times Literary Supplement* for replying to my letter asking for information about D. H. Lawrence's letters and especially Mr. R. W. Gaskell, of the University of Bristol, who provided me with the exact references for these quotations.

[9] These two passages are both quoted from Malraux's *La Condition Humaine* (Gallimard, 1933, p. 68), and are thoughts of Kyo Gisors after his wife May has told him that she has been unfaithful.

Absurd characters.[1]

Caligula. The sword and the dagger.

"I don't think they quite understood me the day before yesterday when I battered the officiating priest over the head with the mallet that he was going to use to kill the heifer. Yet it was very simple. I wanted, just for once, to change the order of things—just to see what happened. And what I saw was that nothing was changed. The spectators were surprised and a little frightened. Apart from that, the sun went down at the same time. The conclusion which I drew was that it doesn't matter if you change the order of things."

But why should not the sun one day rise in the West?

Id. (Ptolemy.) I had him killed because there was no reason for him to display a finer cloak than mine. There

[1] The *cahier* made it quite clear that Caligula, Ptolemy, Quixote, and La Pallice were all "absurd characters." La Pallice (or Pallisse) was a French captain killed at the battle of Pavia in 1525. He was the hero of an old popular song, revived in the eighteenth century, the refrain of which was:

> Monsieur d'La Palice est mort
> Mort devant Pavie
> Un quart d'heure avant sa mort
> Il était encore en vie.

The last couplet was considered very funny, because it stated so obvious a fact, and gave rise to the expression "Vérité de Monsieur de La Pallice" —more or less the equivalent of "Queen Anne's dead." Camus refers to him again at the very beginning of *The Myth of Sisyphus*, p. 4, when he says that there are only two intellectual methods: that of Monsieur de La Pallisse and that of Don Quixote. The contrast seems to be between someone who accepts the things that are obviously and completely true, and someone who completely neglects them. Both, presumably, are equally absurd, though in *The Myth of Sisyphus* Camus writes that it is only by a balance between them that we can "reach at one and the same time both emotion and clarity."

was, in the absolute, no reason at all. Naturally, there was no reason either why my cloak should be finer. But he wasn't aware of this, and since I was the only person who saw things clearly, it was natural for me to benefit from this.

Don Quixote and La Pallice.

La Pallice: "A quarter of an hour before my death, I was still alive. This has sufficed to make me famous. But this is no true claim to glory. My real philosophy is that, a quarter of an hour after my death, I shall no longer be alive."

Don Quixote: "Yes, I have tilted against windmills. Because it doesn't matter in the slightest whether you fight windmills or giants. It matters so little that they are easily confused. My metaphysics are those of the short-sighted."

Vedas: What a man thinks, that does he become.

Gisèle and the war: "No, I don't read the papers. What interests me is the weather. I'm going camping on Sunday."

"Do you know, Fontanes, what most amazes me in the world? The inability of force to maintain anything at all. There are only two powers in the world: the sword and the mind. In the long run, the sword is always defeated by the mind." Napoleon.[2]

[2] Napoleon's remark to Fontanes is repeated at the beginning of *Les Amandiers*, 1940, *L'Eté*, 1954.

Louis XIV: "My child, you are going to become a great king. Do not follow me in my taste for war. Try to ease the lot of your peoples . . . something which I am unfortunate enough not to be able to have done."

Oran [3]

The plain of Le Tlélat as a preparation for Oran. A place for achieving freedom and renouncing desire before plunging into the senses, for withdrawing into meditation before going down into the bliss of hell.

You can travel to Oran either by day or by night. I don't know what happens by day. But by night, I know that you arrive at dawn at Sainte-Barbe du Tlélat, after having passed by the quivering eucalyptus trees of Perrégaux at that doubtful hour which is no longer night but not yet day. At Tlélat, you find that little station with green shutters and its large clock.

. . . But Tlélat, when it rains. . . .

Sainte-Barbe du Tlélat, you who are indifference, equivalence, and freedom, keep us from overhasty choices and leave us that undivided liberty which is called emptiness of the senses. In a few moments, we shall be in Oran, in the heaviness of a life of the body lived without hope. We shall see motionless Santa Cruz and smell the aniseed in the streets of Mers-el-Kébir. There will be the "Vieilles Cures" which the café Cintra serves in powdered ice, and

[3] Most of these passages on Oran were incorporated into *The Minotaur, or the Stop in Oran*, 1940, *L'Eté*, 1954 (tr. O'Brien in *The Myth of Sisyphus*, 1955). However, it should also be noted that *The Plague* is set in Oran, and that a number of Camus's best effects in the novel are obtained by contrasting the dullness of the city with the extraordinary events that take place there.

the women of Oran whose ankles are rather thick and who always go out bareheaded. Sainte-Barbe, preserve these women of Oran until they reach the threshold of old age, and then replace them by many exactly identical women who will also walk under the trees of the old Préfecture. Prevent, O Sainte-Barbe, prevent the women of Oran from thinking of Algiers and of Paris, and teach them the truth of this world, which is that it has none. You who are like a quayside where one dreamily smokes a cigarette, waiting for the blast of a whistle that will speed one again to the landscapes of the earth, you know that I do not often feel religious. But if such a mood does come over me, you know that I have no need of God, and that I can be religious only when I want to play at it, because a train is going to leave and because there will be no tomorrow to my prayer. Sainte-Barbe, you who are a point in space on the line from Algiers to Oran, closer to Oran, very close to Oran, and a pause in the time carrying me to Oran, you who are both so carnal and so punctual, so earthly and so cardinal, be for a brief moment an unbeliever's saint and an innocent's counselor.

Oran. An extravagant town, where shoe shops display ghastly models on plaster casts of tortured feet, where "practical jokes and tricks" lie side by side in shop windows with tricolor wallets, where you can still find extraordinary cafés, their grease-proof counters scattered with the feet and wings of dead flies, where you are served in chipped glasses. Happy cafés of a happy country where a small cup of coffee costs twelve sous and a large one eighteen.

In an antique shop, a vulgar Virgin Mary carved in wood smiles indecently, bearing the name of a famous unknown artist. But underneath it, to dispel any ignorance, the owners have placed a card: "Wooden virgin by Maya." The photographers' shops display astonishing faces, from the Oranais sailor leaning with one elbow on a console table to the oddly clad young lady of marriageable age against a sylvan background, and including the authentic product of Oran, the handsome young man with plastered-down hair and a mouth like an air-raid trench.

Easy and unrivaled city, with its parade of imperfect but touching young girls, their faces free both of make-up and of feigned emotions, whose attempts at coquetry are so charmingly unsuccessful.

Apollo's café, *Melos's Place,* little bars, tramways in the form of gondolas, eighteenth-century pastels leaning against a mechanical donkey in plush velvet, *eau de Provence* for preparing green olives, patriotically colored displays of flowers in the florists' windows—Oran, the Chicago of our absurd Europe.

Santa Cruz hewn out of the rock, the mountains, the flat sea, the sun, and the violent wind, the great cranes, the immense flights of stairs going up the City Rock, the streetcars, bridges, and warehouses—one feels, somehow, that there is a kind of greatness in all this.

I have often heard people from Oran complain: "There's no interesting milieu." But, by heaven, you wouldn't want it if there were! Certain forms of greatness do not inspire elevating thoughts. They are sterile by their very nature, and keep man face to face with his own condition. Leave circles of society alone and go down into the street. (But Oran is not made for the people of Oran.)

Oran. Canastel, and the motionless sea at the foot of the red cliffs. Two immense and sleepy headlands standing out of the clear water. The faint noise of a motorboat coming toward us. And, advancing imperceptibly on the dazzling sea, a coast-guard vessel bathed in radiant light. An overfullness of beauty and indifference—the call of inhuman and glittering forces. On the plateau, exquisitely colored quivering saffron.

The bay of Mers-el-Kébir and the path under the almond trees in full bloom. The perfect shape of the bay—its *average* width—the water like a sheet of blue metal. Indifference.

Id. above the tile factory. Red and blue. Transparency of things. Indifference.

NOVEMBER

When Borgia was elected Pope, a fire of tow was lit three times before him to recall to this master of the world that the world's glory is a fleeting thing.

He dispensed justice "admirably" (Burchard [4]).

[4] The numerous references to the Italian Renaissance which now follow are, for the most part, taken from the *Journal* of Jean Burchard, which, as Camus obligingly tells us, was published by Turmel in 1933 (p. 135).

Innocent VIII, whom a Jewish medium gave woman's milk to drink, mingled with human blood.

Ferdinand of Naples, using the bodies of the enemies he had had tortured and executed "to decorate his apartments."

Alexander and Lucrezia Borgia, who protected the Jews on every occasion. Alexander divided the world between Spaniards and Portuguese by drawing a straight line from the Azores to the South Pole. The world is worth no more than that.

According to Burchard

After the death of his son, the Duke of Gandia, Alexander VI remained stupefied by frenzied suffering. He looked with staring eyes at the bloodstained and motionless corpse—and then shut himself in his room, where he was heard sobbing.

Took no food or drink from Thursday to Saturday, and did not sleep until Sunday.

Cesare Borgia. Strong, suffered from "health accidents," abscesses which kept him in bed, "gloomy forebodings mingled with his youthful glory." Interspersed his work with violent pleasures. Slept by day, worked by night. "Aut Caesar, aut nihil."

NOVEMBER 1939 [5]

Novel. He has achieved and will achieve nothing because he tries to do too many different things, because he can-

[5] Both Meursault and Mersault sleep a lot.

not choose between his various duties, and because one can only create a work of art if. . . .

He can be completely explained by his habits, of which the most deadly is to stay in bed. He can't do anything about it. And what he wants to become, what he admires and dreams about, is exactly the opposite. He longs for a work born of the very opposite of his habits—one born of the resolutions that he makes.

NOVEMBER 1939

It is legitimate to glory in the diversity and quantity of experience—and especially in the life of the senses and the surrender to passionate impulses—only if one is completely disinterested in the object of one's desires.

There is also the leap into material things—and many men who glory in the senses do so only because they are slaves to them. Here, too, they embrace the vulture which is eating them away.

Hence the absolute necessity to have gone through the experience of chastity, for example, and to have been ruthless with oneself. Before any deliberately thought-out enterprise aimed at glorifying the world of immediate experience, a month's asceticism in everything.

Sexual chastity.

Mental chastity—prevent your desires from straying, your thoughts from wandering.

One single, unchanging subject for meditation. Reject everything else.

Work continuously, at a definite time, with no falling off, etc., etc. (Moral training and asceticism too.)

A single moment of weakness and everything collapses, both practice and theory.

At Ferrara, the palace of Schifanoia, built by Alberto d'Este, to "avoid boredom."

The Este.

Hippolytus, who had his brother Giulio's eyes torn out because the woman he loved said that she "preferred Giulio's eyes to Hippolytus's body."

Giulio and Fernando try to murder Hippolytus and Alfonso d'Este. Their plot is discovered, they are sentenced to death, but sadistically pardoned on the scaffold. Thirty-five years in a dungeon for Fernando, who died there, and fifty-four for Giulio, who came out mad.

Alfonso d'Este had a statue of Giulio II by Michelangelo melted down and made into a cannon.

Cf. Gonzague Truc: [6] "They built only for themselves, and because they refused to efface their own personality in the presence of a work of art, humbly ordering it in the direction of the mysterious labor of the universe (?), and nourishing it with eternal values (?), they condemned it to disappear the moment it was born. Their own lives left behind them only haughty and accursed names." *Quite.*

Bibliography for the Borgias.

Louis de Villefosse (*Machiavel et nous*, 1937).

[6] Cf. *Rome et les Borgia* (Grasset, 1939). The question marks are Camus's own, and seem to indicate a certain reluctance to accept so moral a standpoint.

Rafael Sabatini (*César Borgia,* 1937).

Fred Bérence (*Lucrèce Borgia,* '37).

Gab. Brunet (*Ombres vivantes,* '36).

L. Collinson-Morley (*Histoire des Borgia*).

Charles Benoist (*Machiavel*).

The *Journal* of Jean Burchard (edited by Turmel, 1933), etc., etc.

1940

Evenings on the terrace of the *Deux Merveilles*. The moving breast of the sea that can be sensed in the hollowness of the night. The quivering olive trees and the smell of smoke rising from the earth.

The rocks in the sea covered with white seagulls. With their gray mass, lit up by the whiteness of the birds' wings, they look like luminous floating cemeteries.

Novel.[7]

This story, begun on a blue, burning hot beach, in the sunburned bodies of two young creatures—swimming, games in the sun and water—summer evenings on the roads leading to the beaches, with the scent of fruit and smoke in the empty shadows—the body relaxing in light clothes. The attraction between two beings, and the secret, tender bliss in a heart of seventeen.

—Ended up in Paris, with the cold or the gray sky, the

[7] At first sight, it would appear that Camus is talking either about *La Mort Heureuse* or about *The Stranger*. However, it would be unwise to see the whole passage as autobiographical, since Camus was twenty-seven in 1940, not twenty-four.

pigeons among the black stones of the Palais Royal, the city and its lights, rapid kisses, tiring and uneasy tenderness, wisdom and desire rising in the heart of a man of twenty-four—the "let's stay friends."

Id. This other story, begun on a cold and stormy night, lying with my back on the earth under a sky crossed by stars and clouds:

—continued on the hills around Algiers or in front of the wide and mysterious port.

—Poverty-stricken and magnificent Kasbah, the cemetery of El Kettar emptying out all its tombstones toward the sea, warm soft lips among the promegranate trees, and a tomb—trees, hills, the climb to the pure and dried-out Bouzareah, and, turning back to the sea, the taste of lips and our eyes full of sunlight.

It begins not in love but in the desire to live. But is love so far off when, after climbing up through the wind to the great square house above the sea, two bodies cling close together, while from the far horizon the soft breathing of the sea rises to this room cut off from the rest of the world? The marvel of night, when the hope of love is one with the rain, the sky, and the earth's silences. Exact balance of two beings joined together by their bodies, and made alike by a common indifference to everything which is not this moment in the world.

This other moment which is like a dance, she in a period dress and he in a dancer's costume.

The first almond trees in blossom along the road by the sea. One night has been enough for them to be covered with this fragile snow that we cannot imagine standing up to the cold and the rain which drenches all their petals.

In the streetcar.

The old lady with a face like a procuress, but wearing a cross on her nonexistent bosom.

"Honest women know how to behave. Not like the ones who do well out of war. Their husbands gone, they get the allowance, and then they have another man. Why, one of them said to me: 'He can die at the front for all I care. He was a nasty devil before he went into the army. The war's not going to change that.' It was no good my saying: 'Now that he's at the front, you must learn to forgive.' No good at all. But, you know, when they're bad they're like that. It's in their blood, you know, in their blood."

FEBRUARY

Oran. From a long way off, as soon as you get to Valmy, you can see the mountains of Santa Cruz, with the deep gash in the earth and the cathedral itself like a stone finger pointing up into the blue sky.

The thing to do, at the corner of the boulevard Gallieni, is to have your shoes cleaned at ten in the morning. A gentle breeze blows, the sun shines, men and women hurry by, and perched on your high stool, you feel an extraordinary happiness at the sight of the shoeshiners at work. Everything is finished, worked out, minutely organized right down to the last detail. There is a moment when the whole astonishing operation seems to be finished, when you see them using the soft brushes and can gaze on the final gleam of the shoes. But no. The same fanatically enthusiastic hand spreads polish once again over the shining surface, dulls it, rubs it, sends the polish down into the very depths of the hide, and brushes it until the double and truly final shine springs out from the heart of the leather.

The *maison du colon,* which expresses at one and the same time a metaphysical, a moral, and an aesthetic attitude. An elaborate edifice crowned by an Egyptian pschent. A curious mosaic, for some reason in Byzantine style, shows charming nurses, sandals on their feet, carrying cushions piled high with grapes, and a whole procession of natives, clad as nature intended, hurrying toward an elegant settler wearing a topee and a bow tie.

The rue d'Austerlitz and its age-old Jews. Every action is a miniature drama.

Tailors like Marie-Christine are "not only fashionable but always up to date." Laxatives are "only a temporary remedy. The roots of constipation remain untouched." [8]

From the top of the coast road, the cliffs are so thick that the landscape becomes unreal through its very quali-

[8] Meursault also likes to cut out advertisements for laxatives (cf. *The Stranger,* p. 25). The phrase "not only fashionable but always up to date" is in English in the text.

ties. Man is an outlaw there, so much so that all this beauty seems to come from another world.

The tiny Place de la Perle, where the children play at two in the afternoon. Mosque, minarets, benches, a small piece of sky. The chattering of a Spanish radio. What I like here is not this particular hour, but another which I feel exists, when the summer sky loses its heat, the little square softens in the evening, and soldiers and women wander around while the scent of aniseed draws the men into the bars.

Novel about women: One theme. Sincerity.

"Oh my soul, do not aspire to immortal life, but exhaust the limits of the possible." Pindar, *Pythian* iii.[9]

Characters.[1]
The old man and his dog. Eight years of hatred.
The other man, and his verbal mannerism: "He was charming and, moreover, very pleasant."
"A deafening noise and, moreover, one that made you jump."
"It's eternal and, moreover, human."
A.T.R.

[9] The quotation from Pindar was placed at the beginning of *The Myth of Sisyphus*. It is also, it may be noted, used by Paul Valéry to introduce *Le Cimetière Marin*.

[1] These two characters both figure in *The Stranger*, as Salamano and Raymond's friend Masson, respectively. Mme Camus tells me that she does not know what A.T.R. refers to.

A morning spent with bare bodies and sunlight. A shower, then light and heat.

FEBRUARY

This Florentine countenance which tells of its love and tormented past. How much of its expression is play-acting? And also, how much is real emotion, so great and overwhelming at certain moments, so slight at others?

Maria—like the soul of Paris. This morning spent in the sun, and the town full of lights—her eyes like the town, and this easy life. "*O dolore dei tuoi martiri, o diletto del tuo amore.*"

"It is not love that she represents, but a chance for life—everything that is not exile, everything that says 'yes' to life. And never was a chance for life given so touching a face. Who can be sure that he is in love? But everyone can recognize emotion. This song, this face, this deep and supple voice, this free and expertly planned life, is all I hope for or expect. And if I give up, these visions nevertheless remain as so many promises of freedom, and as this image of myself from which I cannot break loose."

MARCH [2]

What does this sudden awakening mean, in this dark room, with the sounds of a city that has suddenly become foreign to me? And everything is foreign to me, everything, with-

[2] The translation of *étranger* by "foreign" is unavoidable but misleading. In French, the reference to the title and atmosphere of *The Stranger* —and to the opening pages of *The Myth of Sisyphus*—is obvious.

out a single person who belongs to me, with no hiding place to heal this wound. What am I doing here, what is the point of these smiles and gestures? My home is neither here nor elsewhere. And the world has become merely an unknown landscape where my heart can lean on nothing. Foreign—who can know what this word means?

Foreign, admit that I find everything strange and foreign.

Now that everything is clear-cut, wait and spare nothing. At least, work in such a way as to achieve both silence and literary creation. Everything else, everything, whatever may happen, is unimportant.

Evening: Events. Characters. Personal reactions.

Trouville. A plateau, covered with asphodels, facing the sea. Little villas with green or white gates, some buried under tamarisks, a few others bare and surrounded by stones. A slight complaint rises from the sea. But everything, the sun, the slight breeze, the whiteness of the asphodels, the already hard blue of the sky, brings to mind the summer, the gilded youth of its daughters and sunburned suns, passions coming to life, long hours in the sun, and the sudden softness of the evenings. What other meaning can we find to our days but this, and the lesson we draw from this plateau: a birth, a death, and, between the two, beauty and melancholy?

R. C. The kind of man who gives the impression that he hides to go to the lavatory. But then, you find that they have developed a theory about it, and that man's greatness lies in being aware of what humbles him. And, immediately, it is we who feel disgusted.

S. who wants to write the diary of a novel which remained unwritten by its author.

More and more,[3] when faced with the world of men, the only reaction is one of individualism. Man alone is an end unto himself. Everything you try to do for the common good ends in failure. Even if you like to try it from time to time, decency demands that you do so with the required amount of scorn. Withdraw into yourself completely, and play your own game (Idiotic).

The man who receives a letter from his mistress's husband. In it, the husband proclaims his love, and confesses that, before giving way completely to his anger, he would like to speak directly to his rival. What the lover is afraid of is anger. Consequently, he is full of admiration for the husband's generous impulse. And the more afraid he is, the more he says this. He insists. This gives him the best part to play. He will give up everything, simply out of gratitude for this generous impulse, he will sacrifice himself—without a murmur—since he is unworthy compared

[3] The word "IDIOT" was written across this remark in red pencil by Camus himself.

171

to the husband. Moreover, he partly believes all this. But we must also take into account his fear of being hit.

A dog in the house. S. makes it welcome, in spite of his mother. The dog steals two anchovies. The mother chases him, and the dog runs away, terrified, while S. says: "Don't run away, don't be frightened."

Afterwards, S.: "Poor dog, he thought he was already in heaven."

His mother: "Yes, I've believed in heavens too, but I've never seen them in my lifetime."

S.: "Yes, but he was there already."

Journey down to the sea from above Mers-el-Kébir. The line of hills and cliffs surrounding the bay. My heart closed to all this.

Marseilles. The fair: Life? Nothingness? Illusions? But truth none the less? Big drum. Boom, boom, come into Nothingness.

At the dawn of modern times: All is fulfilled? [4] Right —then let us start to live.

PARIS. MARCH 1940

What is hateful in Paris: tenderness, feelings, a hideous sentimentality that sees everything beautiful as pretty and

[4] Perhaps a reference to John: xix: 30, except that the wording in the most frequently used French Bible, the Segond, is: "Tout est accompli," and Camus writes: "Tout est consommé." If it is a Biblical quotation, then it is yet another indication of the Nietzschean climate of Camus's early thought.

everything pretty as beautiful. The tenderness and despair that accompany the murky skies, the shining roofs
and endless rain.

What is inspiring: the terrible loneliness. As a remedy to
life in society, I would suggest the big city. Nowadays, it
is the only desert within our means. Here, the body has
lost its magic. It is covered over, and hidden under shape-
less skins. The only thing left is the soul, the soul with all
its sloppy overflow of drunken sentimentality, its whining
emotions and everything else. But the soul also offers us
one source of greatness: silent solitude. When you look at
Paris from the Butte Montmartre, seeing it like a monstrous cloud of steam beneath the rain, a gray and shape-
less swelling on the surface of the earth, and then turn
to look at the Calvary of Saint-Pierre de Montmartre, you
can feel the kinship between a country, an art, and a religion. Every line of these stones, and every one of these
scourged or crucified bodies is quivering with the same
wanton and defiled emotion as the town itself, and is
pouring it into men's hearts.

But, on the other hand, the soul is never right, and here
less than elsewhere. For the most splendid expressions
which it has given to this soul-obsessed religion have been
hewn out of stone in imitation of bodily forms. And if this
god touches you, it is because his face is that of a man.
It is a strange limitation of the human condition that it
should be unable to escape from humanity, and that it
should have to clothe in bodies those of its symbols which
try to deny the body. They do deny it, but it gives them
their titles to greatness. Only the body is generous. And
we feel that this Roman legionary is alive because of his

extraordinary nose or hunched back, this Pilate because of the expression of ostentatious boredom that stone has preserved for him over the centuries.

From this point of view, Christianity has understood. And if it has made so deep an impact on us, it is by its God who was made man. But its truth and greatness come to an end on the cross, at the moment when this man cries out that he has been forsaken. If we tear out the last pages of the New Testament, then what we see set forth is a religion of loneliness and human grandeur. Certainly, its bitterness makes it unbearable. But that is its truth, and all the rest is a lie.[5]

Hence the fact that being able to live alone in one room in Paris for a year teaches a man more than a hundred literary salons and forty years' experience of "Parisian life." It is a hard, terrible, and sometimes agonizing experience, and always on the verge of madness. But, by being close to such a fate, a man's quality must either become hardened and tempered—or perish. And if it perishes, then it is because it was not strong enough to live.

Eisenstein [6] and Mexican death festivals.

Ghoulish masks to amuse the children, sugar skulls that they nibble at with delight. The children play with death,

[5] An indication of Camus's attitude toward Christianity which was already partly expressed in a leading article in *Soir-Républicain*, where he wrote, on January 1, 1940: "There was a night in the history of humanity when a man weighed down with all his destiny looked at his sleeping companions and, alone in a silent world, declared that no one must sleep, but that all must watch to the end of time. We are still living in times like these."

[6] Camus had probably been to see *Time in the Sun* (*Qué viva México*).

finding it funny, finding it sweet and sugary. Likewise the "little dead ones." Everything leads up to "Our friend Death."

Paris

The woman from the floor above has killed herself by jumping into the courtyard of the hotel. She was thirty-one, said one of the tenants. Old enough to live, and, since she had lived a little, to die. The shadow of the drama still lingers on in the hotel. She sometimes used to come down and ask the owner's wife to let her stay for supper. She suddenly used to kiss her—from a need to feel another person's warmth and presence. It ended with a three-inch split in her forehead. Before she died she said: "At last."

Paris

The black trees against the gray sky, and the sky-blue pigeons. The statues on the grass, and this melancholy elegance.

The pigeons fly away with a sound like clothes flapping on a line. You hear them cooing in the green grass.

Paris

The little cafés at five in the morning—their windows steamed over—boiling hot coffee—the people who work in the markets and who bring in the food—the little morning glass of liqueur, and Beaujolais later on.

Léger.[7] Intelligence—and this metaphysical painting which rethinks matter. Odd: as soon as one starts to re-think matter, the only thing that turns out to be perma-nent is what made it look as it did: color.

The man in a restaurant who hears a woman calling him up and giving his name and telephone number. *He* replies from the other end. She talks *to him* as if he were there (about his family, with precise details and so on). He doesn't understand. That's how things are.

No future.
"The works here mentioned by J. M. have been burned. But he could, naturally, have just as easily published them, and they would have contained only contradictions or matters of no concern, which amounts to the same thing." S. L.

To give punctuation and regularity of breathing, note down all the events of my life: "Today, I am twenty-seven," and so on.

Have a system of notes by a commentator—or a preface which sums up.

[7] This note recurs in *The Myth of Sisyphus*, p. 99, where Camus re-marks that "the most intellectual kind of painting, the one that tries to re-duce reality to its essential elements, is ultimately but a visual delight. All it has kept of the world is its color."

The little Spanish soldier in the restaurant. Not a word of French, and this desire for human warmth when he talks to me. A peasant from Estremadura, fought on the Republican side, was in Argelès concentration camp, joined the French Army. When he says the word "Spain," the whole sky of his native country leaps into his eyes. Has a week's leave. Has come to Paris, which has reduced him to pulp in a few hours. Wandering in the métro, not speaking a word of French, a foreigner, foreign to everything that is not his own country, his joy would be to find the friends from his own regiment again. So that even if he is to die under low clouds, in thick mud, it will at least be by the side of men from his own country.

APRIL

At The Hague. The man who lives in a boardinghouse without knowing that it is a brothel. Never anyone in the dining room. He comes down in his dressing gown. Enter a gentleman in morning coat and top hat. He is stiff, punctilious, and black. He asks for a very good meal. The dove coos in the dining-room cage. Then the man departs, leaving the price of the meal on the table. Sudden silence. The waiter comes back and goes into a panic. The Negro has taken the dove away under his opera hat.

Novel (Part II—consequences).

The man (J. C.) has picked such and such a day on which to die—fairly soon. His immediate and astonishing superiority over all social and other forces.

The little soldier in the métro. About forty. Tries to arrange a meeting with a fairly young girl. "Perhaps I might drop in one day if I came that way." "Oh no, my brother would be cross." "Oh, yes, of course, naturally, you're quite right. But could I write to you?" "No, I'd rather meet you." This direct acceptance of his roundabout suggestion overwhelms him. "Yes, right, very good. Yes, you're quite right, that's much better. Well now, let's think. Tomorrow's Monday. Yes, that's right, Monday. Now, about what time? I have to think about it, you see, because in this kind of job. . . . Well now, yes, Monday's tomorrow. Well, what about five o'clock?"

She (still direct): "After dinner?"

He (still left behind): "Yes, yes, that'll be fine, very good."

She: "Eight o'clock."

He: "Yes, yes, eight o'clock. At the Terrace, if that's all right."

She: "Yes."

He stops talking. But suddenly you can feel him starting to panic but not admitting it. He needs to make sure that the chance of an adventure that has become so easy and so precious does not escape. "And if something went wrong, could I write to you?" "No, I'd rather you didn't." "Well, we could set another time, in case you couldn't come on Monday." "Yes, Thursday at the same place." This reassures him, but he is suddenly afraid that this new arrangement will take some importance from tomorrow's. "But, in any case, eight o'clock tomorrow, without fail. It's only in case something should go wrong." "Yes," she replies. She gets off at Concorde and he at Saint-Lazare.

An artist who goes to Port-Cros in order to paint. And everything is so beautiful that he buys a house, puts his paintings away, and never touches them again.

At *Paris-Soir* you feel the whole heart of Paris and its despicable shopgirl values. Mimi's garret has become a skyscraper, but her heart is still the same. Rotten with sentimentality, prettiness, self-indulgence, all the sticky refuges which man uses to defend himself in so harsh a town.

You would not write about loneliness so much if you knew how to get the most out of it.

"I," he said, "am an olfactive type. And there is no art that addresses itself to the sense of smell. Only life."

Short story. A priest, happy with his lot in a country parish in Provence. By accident, has to succor a man sentenced to death just before his execution. Loses his faith because of it.

Preface to Terracini: [8] "There are many of us who feel the same nostalgia for this sense of exile. These lands of

[8] Probably Enrico Terracini, an Italian diplomat in 1909, the author of two books published in Algiers by Charlot, Camus's first publisher: *D'un soir, d'un pays lointain,* and *Les Miens.* The second was translated by Jacques Heurgon, the writer to whom Camus dedicated the essay *Summer in Algiers* in *The Myth of Sisyphus.*

Spain and Italy have given their form to so many European souls that they belong a little to Europe themselves, to this Europe of the mind that will triumph over all those welded together by force of arms. It is here, perhaps, that the meaning of these pages is to be found. For this reason, they were already modern two hundred years ago. They remain so today. And we must not lose hope that their youth will still be alive on the day when flowers grow again out of the ruins."

Second series. For Don Juan.[9] See Larousse: the Franciscan monks killed him and pretended that he had been struck dead by the Commander. Last act. Speeches of the Franciscans to the people: "Don Juan has been converted," etc. "Glory to Don Juan."

Second to last act: Don Juan challenges the Commander, who does not turn up. The bitterness of being right.

Second series. For Don Juan.

(Don Juan and the Franciscan father go into Don Juan's entrance hall, and Don Juan accompanies the monk to the door.)

Opening.

The Franciscan: "So, Don Juan, you believe in nothing?"

Don Juan: "No, Father, I believe in three things."

[9] Don Juan fascinated Camus during his whole life, and is said to have been the hero of a play which Camus was preparing when he was killed. The phrase about the bitterness of being right occurs in *The Myth of Sisyphus*, p. 76, where Don Juan is studied as one of the "absurd men."

The Franciscan: "And may one know what these are?"

Don Juan: "I believe in courage, intelligence, and women."

The Franciscan: "Then we must give up all hope for you."

Don Juan: "Yes, if you must pity a man who is happy. Good-bye, Father."

The Franciscan (at the door): "I shall pray for you, Don Juan."

Don Juan: "Thank you, Father. I like to look on prayer as a form of courage."

The Franciscan (gently): "No, Don Juan, it is simply a matter of two feelings that you insist on misunderstanding: charity and love."

Don Juan: "I know only tenderness and generosity, which are the manly forms of these female virtues. But farewell, Father."

The Franciscan: "Farewell."

M A Y

The Stranger is finished.

What an admirable play *Le Misanthrope* is, with its crude contrasts and its typed characters.[1]

Alceste and Philinte

Célimène and Eliante

The monotony of Alceste—the absurd consistency of a character pushed to its logical conclusion—which is

[1] The remark about *Le Misanthrope* recurs in *The Myth of Sisyphus*, p. 82, as an illustration of the absurd destiny of the actor.

the whole theme of the play. And the line of poetry, the "bad line," with about as little scansion in it as the monotony of the main character.

The exodus from Paris.

Clermont. The lunatic asylum and its curious clock. The dirt of the five-o'clock dawns. The blind patients—the madman in the block who screams all day—this earth on a small scale. The whole body turned in the direction of two poles, the sea or Paris. It is at Clermont that one can get to know Paris.

SEPTEMBER

Finished the first part of The Absurd.

The man who razes his house to the ground, burns his fields, and covers them with salt so as not to surrender them.

Little man from the Banque de France. Transferred to Clermont, tries to keep the same habits. Almost succeeds. But is just very slightly out of tune.

OCTOBER 1940. LYONS

Saint Thomas (himself one of Frédèric's subjects) acknowledges that subjects have the right to revolt. Cf. Baumann, *Politique de Saint Thomas*, p. 136.

The last of the Carraras, a prisoner in a Padua emptied
by the plague and besieged by the Venetians, strode
through all the rooms of his palace shouting at the top of
his voice: he was calling on the devil and asking him for
death.[2]

At Siena, a condottiere saves the city. He asks for
everything. The people argue thus: "Nothing will ever reward him sufficiently, not even absolute power. Let us kill
him. Afterwards, we will worship him." Which they did.

Gian-Paulo Baglioni, of whom Machiavelli says that he
missed the chance of rendering himself immortal when he
missed that of killing Pope Julius II.

Burchard: "Villainy, impiety, military talent, and intellectual culture could all be found in J. Malatesta" (died
1417).

Filippo-Maria Visconti, condottiere of Milan, forbade
people to talk about death in his presence and asked that
his favorites be taken out of his sight when they were
dying. And yet Burchard tells us: "He died with dignity
and nobility."

At Dante's tomb, at Ravenna, the people took the candles
from the holy altar to honor him: "Thou art more
worthy than the other, the one they crucified."

Short story: Follow the Rhône and Saône along their
course, see the first leap ahead, the other hesitate but
finally join up again and lose itself in its headlong rush.
One person goes down each of them: parallel.

[2] Cf. *The Myth of Sisyphus*, p. 90. Camus there continues: "It was a
means of surmounting it."

Story of Y.

Ternay. Cold, forsaken little village overhanging the Rhône. A gray sky, and a wind as cold as a shantung dress. The uplands left fallow. A few black furrows with crows flying above them. A little cemetery open to the heavens: they were all good husbands and fathers. They all leave eternal regrets.

The old church with a copy of a painting by Boucher. The woman who looks after the chairs: she was so afraid when the German bombers came. The village had already had thirty men killed in the last war. Now, there are only eighteen prisoners, but it's hard all the same. Two young people are going to be married soon. The schoolmistress is a refugee from Alsace, who has had no news from her parents. "Do you think it's going to end soon?" The chair-attendant's son was killed in '14, she went to get him when he was wounded, and was near the retreat from the Marne. She brought him back home, where he died. "I shall never forget what I saw."

Outside, the same sky and the same cold. The plowed fields are just warm, and down below the river is flat and shiny, with the occasional ripple. A little farther on, the waiting room of a little station at Serresin. Wartime lighting—a shadow on the notice inviting people to lead a happy life at Bandol. The stove has gone out, and the figure eights made by the water sprinkled there by the street cleaners look like tracings on the cold flagstones. An hour to wait with the trains rumbling in the distance and the evening wind in the valley. So cut off and so near. Here, you actually touch your liberty and feel how atrocious it is. Linked, linked forever to this world where the flowers and the wind will never make us forgive all the rest.

DECEMBER

(Egypt)
The Greeks—the Etruscans—Rome and its decadence—the Alexandrians and the Christians—The Holy Roman Empire and the audacity of its thought—Provence and the Provençal schisms—the Italian Renaissance—the Elizabethan period—Spain—from Goethe to Nietzsche —Russia.

India, China, Japan.

Mexico—the United States.

Styles of architecture—from the Doric column to the concrete arch through Gothic and Baroque.

History Philosophy Art Religion.

P.S.M.

DECEMBER

The Greeks. History—Literature—Art—Philosophy.

Consciously or not, women always make use of this feeling for honor and respect for promises which is so intense among men.

Cain's sons [3]—as they were. The father watches Abel's murder and does nothing about it. But Cain grows in suffering and in strength. The father offers forgiveness, which Cain refuses. "I no longer want to see your face."

(Or else a poem—*id*. Judah.)

ORAN. JANUARY 1941

Story of P.[4] The little old man who throws scraps of paper down from the balcony to attract the cats. Then spits on them. When he hits one, the old man laughs.

There is nowhere that the people of Oran have not disfigured by some hideous piece of building that ought by rights to destroy any landscape. A town which turns its back on the sea and then turns around on itself like a snail. You wander through this labyrinth, looking for the sea as for Ariadne's thread. But you turn around and around in these awkward and ugly streets. Finally the Oranais are devoured by the Minotaur: boredom.

But it is all in vain. One of the most powerful lands in the world bursts open the clumsy décor with which men have tried to cover it, and makes its violent cries heard between every house and over all the rooftops. And the life which can be lived above the boredom in Oran is like this

[3] Surely Camus means Adam's. The phrase "I no longer want to see your face" may be Camus's version of Genesis: iv: 14.
[4] Recurs in Tarrou's notebooks in *The Plague*.
Most of these remarks were incorporated into Camus's essay on Oran.

land. Oran proves that there is something stronger in men than their works.

You cannot know what stone is if you have never been to Oran. In one of the dustiest cities in the world, the pebble and the stone are king. Elsewhere, Arab cemeteries have their accustomed charm. Here, above the ravine of Raz el Aïn, facing the sea, these cemeteries are fields of crumbling, blinding white, chalky stone. In the midst of these bones of the earth, the occasional red geranium grows, looking like new blood and life.

Books are written about Florence and Athens. These towns have formed so many European minds that there must be a meaning to be found in them. They can calm or excite, and satisfy a certain hunger of the soul which feeds on memories. But no one would have the idea of writing about a town where there is nothing to attract the mind, where ugliness has played an overwhelming role, and where the past is reduced to nothing. And yet there is sometimes a temptation to do so.

What makes us grow fond of and interested in what has nothing to offer us? What attracts us about this emptiness, this ugliness, and this boredom under a magnificent and implacable sky? My reply is: human beings. There is a certain race of men for whom human beings, wherever they are beautiful, offer a country with a thousand capitals. Oran is a country like this.

Café. Lobsters, sticks of meat, snails served with a sauce that takes the roof off your mouth. You then cool it with a sweet, sickly muscat wine. Things like that aren't just invented. At the side, a blind man is singing flamenco.

The hills above Mers-el-Kébir as a perfect landscape.

Servitude et grandeurs militaires. An admirable book, that one must reread as a man.

"Montecuculli, who withdrew from war after Turenne had been killed, not deigning to match himself against an ordinary player."

Honor is "a wholly human virtue, which one can consider as born of death, with no celestial palm promised after death. It is the virtue of life."

Oran. The ravine of Noiseux: a long path between two dry and dusty slopes. The earth cracks under the sun. The lentisks are the color of stone. The sky above regularly pours down its supply of heat and fire. Little by little, the lentisks start to grow and become green. At first, the vegetation swells almost imperceptibly, then surprisingly fast. At the end of a very long road, the lentisks gradually turn into oak trees, everything becomes bigger and softer almost at the same moment. Then suddenly, coming around a corner, you see a field of almond trees in full blossom: it is like a drink of cool water for the eyes. A little valley like a lost paradise.

The road along the side of the hill, looking over the sea. Still usable, but abandoned. Now it is covered with flowers. Daisies and buttercups make it into a road of yellow and white.

FEBRUARY 21, 1941

Finished *Sisyphus*. The three absurds are now complete.[5] Beginnings of liberty.

MARCH 15, 1941

In the train: "You knew Camps, didn't you?"

"Camps? Tall, thin chap with a black mustache?"

"Yes, he was switchman at Bel-Abbès."

"Yes, of course."

"He's dead."

"Oh? What of?"

"Chest."

"Well, he didn't look like that."

"Yes, but he went in for music, with the male-voice choir. Always blowing away, killed him in the end."

"Well, yes, of course. When you're ill you've got to look after yourself. Mustn't go blowing into a cornet."

[5] The other two absurds are, one assumes, *Caligula* and *The Stranger*, since *The Misunderstanding*, classed by some critics as an "absurd work" had not yet been completed. In the *cahier*, two pages were left blank after this entry in order to emphasize the idea of "beginnings of liberty." Significantly enough, the next entry is a conversation later used in *The Plague*, p. 23.

This entry is to be compared to a later one, on March 7, 1951, when Camus wrote: "Completed the first version of *The Rebel*. This book brings to an end the first two cycles. 37 years old. And now, can creation be free?" In both cases, he seems to have looked upon the completion of a particular "cycle" of works almost as a duty, and to have looked forward to a future period when he no longer felt obliged to write a particular type of book.

The woman who looked as if she had been constipated for three years: "Oh, these Arabs, they still make their girls cover their faces. Oh, they're not civilized yet."

Little by little, she lets us see what her idea of civilization is: a husband earning 1200 francs a month, a two-room apartment, kitchen and bath, the movies every Sunday, and furniture from the Galeries Barbès for weekdays.

The Absurd and Power—develop (cf. Hitler).

MARCH 18, 1941

In spring, the hills around Algiers are overflowing with flowers. The little streets run with the scent of honey from the yellow roses. From the top of enormous black cypress trees spring out bursts of wistaria and hawthorn blossom, their branches hidden inside. A gentle wind, and the immense, flat bay. Strong and simple desire—and the absurdity of leaving all that.

Santa Cruz and the ascent through the pine trees. As you go up, the bay grows wider and wider until, at the very top, your eyes cannot take in its immensity. Indifference—and I too have my pilgrimages.

MARCH 19

Every year, the young girls come into flower on the beaches. They have only one season. The following year, they are replaced by other flower-like faces which, the previous season, still belonged to little girls. For the man who looks at them, they are yearly waves whose weight and splendor break into foam over the yellow beach.

MARCH 20

On Oran. Write an insignificant and absurd biography. On Cain, the insignificant nonentity who carved the insignificant lions in the parade ground.

MARCH 21

The icy water of springtime sea bathing. The dead jellyfish on the beach. Jelly gradually being absorbed into the sand. The enormous dunes of pale sand. Sea and sand— these two deserts.

The weekly paper *Gringoire* suggests that the Spanish refugee camps be transferred to the extreme south of Tunisia.

Give up the tyranny of female charm.

Rosanov: "Michelangelo and Leonardo built something. The revolution will tear out their tongue and slaughter them at the age of twelve or thirteen as soon as they show their own personality, their own soul."

"Deprived of what is sin, man could not live; he would live only too well, deprived of what is holy." Immortality is an idea without a future.

Sakyamuni [6] lived for many years in the desert, motionless, with his eyes turned toward the heavens. The gods themselves envied this wisdom and destiny of stone. In his stiff and outstretched hands, the swallows had made their nests. But one day they flew off, forever. And the man who had killed in himself all will and desire, all glory and pain, began to weep. Thus flowers grow out of stones.

"They may torture but shall not subdue me."

Abbot: "And why not live and act with other men?"
Manfred: "Because my nature was averse to life."

On what should the heart base its actions? Love? Nothing is less reliable. We can know what the pains of love are like, but not love itself. Here, it is deprivation, regret, and empty hands. I shall never have the courage; I am left

---

[6] Cf. *The Minotaur, or the Stop in Oran*, p. 181 in *The Myth of Sisyphus*. The phrase "They may torture but shall not subdue me" is quoted in English in the French text.

The quotation from Act III, scene I, of *Manfred* was rather oddly translated in the version quoted by Camus—or, it may be, in his own translation from the English text. It reads, translated literally back into English:

> But why not live, why not act with men?
> Because their existence revolts my soul.

with anguish. A hell where everything presupposes paradise. It is hell, nevertheless. What I call life and love is
whatever leaves me empty. Departure, constraint,
breaches of love or friendship, my heart scattered in
darkness within me, this salt taste of tears and love.

The wind, one of the few clean things in the world.

APRIL. SECOND SERIES
The world of tragedy and the spirit of revolt.
—Budejovice (3 acts).[7]
Plague or adventure (novel).

The liberating plague [8]
Happy town. People live according to different systems.
The plague: abolishes all systems. But they die all the
same. Doubly useless. A philosopher is writing an "an-
thology of insignificant actions." He will keep a diary of
the plague, from this point of view. (Another diary, this
time from the point of view of the suffering involved. A
classics teacher. He realizes that he had not understood
Thucydides and Lucretius until then. His favorite phrase:
"In all probability." "The streetcar company had only 760
workers available instead of 2,130. In all probability, this
is due to the plague.")

[7] The first version of *The Misunderstanding*, which, according to this
entry, belongs to the "second cycle" of Camus's work (that of revolt)
rather than to the first (that of the absurd).

[8] These notes for *The Plague* were first printed in *Symposium*. The
most insignificant character becomes Grand, the clerk.

A young priest loses his faith at the sight of the black pus flowing out of the wounds. He takes his holy oil away. "If I get out alive. . . ." But he does not. Everything must be paid for.

The bodies are taken away in streetcars. Whole strings of cars, filled with flowers and dead bodies, drive along the cliffs. They immediately fire all the conductors: the passengers no longer pay.

The agency "Ransdoc-S.V.P." (Information Please), gives all information on the telephone. "Two hundred victims today. A charge of two francs will be added to your telephone bill." "Impossible, I'm afraid, no more coffins for four days. Consult the Transport Authority. A charge. . . ." The agency advertises on the radio. "Do you want to know the daily, weekly, or monthly number of plague victims? Phone "Information Please"—six lines: 253–91 to 253–96."

The town gates are closed. People die cut off from the world and packed together. One gentleman, however, keeps to his habits. He continues to dress for dinner. One by one, the members of his family disappear from the table. He dies with his meal in front of him, still dressed for dinner. As the maid says: "Well, there's something to be said for it. We don't need to get him ready for the funeral." They stop burying the dead, and throw them into the sea. But there are too many of them. It's like a monstrous foam on the blue sea.

A man loves a woman and reads the signs of the plague on her face. Never has he loved her so much, and never has he been so disgusted by her. He is divided against himself. But it is always the body that wins. Disgust prevails. He takes her by the hand, drags her from the bed, into the room, the hall, the corridor of the apartment house, through two side streets into the main road. He leaves her near a sewer. "After all, there are other women."

At the end, the most insignificant character decides to speak: "In a way," he says, "it's a disaster."

In the meantime: essay on Oran. The Greeks.

The whole effort of Western art is to provide our imagination with types. And the history of European literature seems to be nothing but a series of variations on the same types and themes. Racinian love is a variation on a type of love which is perhaps never found in life. It is a simplification, a style. The West does not recount the events of everyday life. It is forever feeding its frenzy on great images. It wants to be Manfred or Faust, Don Juan or Narcissus. But it never quite manages to make itself coincide with these images. It is always carried away by the fever for unity. In desperation, it has invented the movie hero.

The sand dunes facing the sea. The faint heat of early dawn, and our bodies stripped bare before the little waves, still bitter and dark with night. The sea lies heavily on the body, which is renewed and runs on to the beach in the first rays of sunlight. Every summer morning on the beach feels like the first morning of the world, and every evening like its solemn ending. Evenings on the sea knew no restraint. The sunbaked days on the sand dunes were overwhelming. At two in the afternoon, you feel drunk after walking a hundred yards along the burning sand. In a moment you feel you will fall and be slain by the sun. In the morning, the beauty of brown bodies against the yellow sand. The terrible innocence of games on the beach and bare bodies in the bounding light.

At night, the dunes turn white under the moon. A little earlier, the evening brings out all the colors, makes them deeper and more violent. The sea is ultramarine, the road red, the color of clotted blood, the beach yellow. Everything disappears as the green sun goes down, and the dunes glisten with moonlight. Nights of limitless happiness under a rain of stars. Is it another body that we hold in our arms, or the soft warmth of the night? And then the night of the storm, when flashes of lightning grew paler as they ran along the dunes, and put an orange or whitish color on the sand and in our eyes. These are nuptials that can never be forgotten. To be able to write: I have been happy for a whole week.

We must pay and dirty ourselves with the meanness of human suffering. The dirty, repulsive, and slimy universe of pain.

"A low moan mingled with sobs was all that could be heard over the sea, until dark-faced night put an end to everything" (The Persians—battle of Salamis).

In 477, to consecrate the Federation of Delos, blocks of iron were cast into the depths of the sea. The oath of alliance was to be kept for as long as the metal remained underwater.

Men have not been sufficiently aware, in politics, of how some kinds of equality are enemies of liberty. In Greece, there were free men because there were slaves.

"It is always a great crime to deprive a people of its liberty on the pretext that it is using it wrongly." (Tocqueville.)

The problem in art is a problem of translation. Bad authors are those who write with reference to an inner context which the reader cannot know. You need to be two people when you write. Once again, the first thing is to learn to govern yourself.

War manuscripts, from prisoners or fighting men. They have all been close to unspeakable experiences, and have drawn nothing from them. Six months working in a post office would have taught them no more. They parrot the papers. What they have read has made a much deeper impression than what they have seen with their own eyes.

"Now is the moment when we should prove by our actions that man's dignity is in no way inferior to the greatness of the gods." (*Iphigenia in Tauris.*)

"I want empire and possession. Action is everything, glory nothing." (*Faust.*)

The world is no secret for the wise man. Why does he need to stray into eternity?

Will is also loneliness.

Liszt on Chopin: "He now used his art only to perform his own tragedy for himself."

SEPTEMBER

Everything is decided. It is simple and straightforward. But then human suffering intervenes, and alters all our plans.

An overwhelming impulse to cast ourselves away and reject everything, to become like nothing at all, utterly destroying what makes us what we are, offering the present only solitude and nothingness, and returning to the only platform where our destinies can suddenly be renewed. The temptation is a permanent one. Should we resist or give way? Is it possible to live a monotonous, repetitive life while perpetually haunted by the thought of a work to be created, or should we adjust our life to this work, follow the lightning flash? It is my concern for beauty, and for liberty, which causes me most anguish.

J. Copeau: "You must look for the playwright, in periods of great artistic creation, not in his study but in the theater, surrounded by his actors. He is both an actor and a producer."

We are not in a period of great artistic creation.

On the Greek theater:
G. Meautis: *Eschyle et la Trilogie.*
L'aristocratie athénienne.
Navarre: *Le théâtre grec.*

In pantomime, strolling players use an incomprehensible language (an esperanto of farce) not for what it means but for the sake of life.

Chancerel is quite right to insist upon the importance of mime. The body in the theater: the whole contemporary French theater (except for Barrault) has forgotten it.

Constitution of the Zibaldone in the *commedia dell' arte.* (Louis Moland: *Molière et la Comédie italienne.*) (Curtain of trimmed cloth.)

Molière, on the point of death, has himself carried to the theater, not wanting to deprive the actors, musicians, and stagehands "who had only their wages to live on" of their share of the takings.

Chancerel's book—interesting in spite of one defect: it might discourage readers. Significant also to see a man preoccupied with the moral influence of the theater never-

theless recommending a list of plays including the Elizabethans. We have lost the habit of this kind of intelligence.

Opinion of Nicholas Clément, Louis XIV's librarian, on
Shakespeare: "This English poet had quite a good imagination, and expresses himself with some skill; but these
fine qualities are hidden by the filth which he puts into
his plays."

The "great century" achieved greatness only by a mutila-
tion of the body and soul, of which this remark is an illustration. During this time, the English poet was writing
magnificently, in *Richard II*:

"Let's talk of graves, of worms and epitaphs."

And Webster wrote:

"Man, like to cassia, is proved best being bruis'd." [9]

Masques, amusements for particular occasions. On the
floor, the dancers followed the pattern made by the initials
of the couple whose marriage the feast was held to cele-
brate.

"Oh! no, there is not the end; the end is death and
madness." (Kyd: *The Spanish Tragedy*.) And at thirty

[9] Cf. Webster: *Duchess of Malfi*, Act III, scene V. Translated directly
back into English, Camus's quotation of it in French reads: "A man is like
cassia; to bring out his smell, you need to bruise him."

Marlowe died of a dagger wound in the forehead, killed by a cop.

Fifty-three manuscript plays of the Warburton collection (Philip Massinger and Fletcher) burned by a head cook who used them to wrap his pies in. That is how it ends.

Cf. Georges Conne: *Le Mystère shakespearien* (Boivin).
Etat présent des études shakespearien-nes (Didier).

OCTOBER

Plague. Bonsels, pp. 144 and 222.

1342—The Black Death in Europe. The Jews are murdered.

1481—The plague ravages the South of Spain. The Inquisition says: The Jews. But the plague kills an inquisitor.

In the second century, discussion about Christ's personal appearance. Saint Cyril and Saint Justin: to give all its meaning to the incarnation, it was maintained that Christ must have looked mean and disgusting. (Saint Cyril: "the most hideous of the sons of men.")

But the Greek attitude was: "If he is not handsome, he is not God." The Greeks won.

On the Cathari: Douais: *Les Hérétiques du Midi au XIII siècle.*

La hermosa Sembra. Denounces her father for plotting against the Inquisition, since she has a Castilian lover and they are "conversos." She goes into a convent. Obsessed with physical desires, she leaves it. Has several children. Grows ugly. Dies with a grocer as her "protector." Asks that her skull be put above the door of the house to remind people of her wicked life. At Seville.

Alexander Borgia was the first to come into conflict with Torquemada. Too knowing and "distinguished" to stand this fury.

See Herder. Ideas to use in a philosophy of the History of Humanity.

Men who have created works of art in periods of great historical disturbances: Shakespeare, Milton, Ronsard, Rabelais, Montaigne, Malherbe.

Initially, the Germans had no feeling for themselves as a nation. What took the place of this was a racial consciousness that was wholly made up by the intellectuals. *Much more virulent.* What interests the Germans is foreign policy—and the French, home policy.

On Monotony.
Monotony of Tolstoy's last works. Monotony of Hindu books—of the Biblical prophets—of Buddha. Monotony

of the Koran, of all religious books. Monotony of Nietzsche —of Pascal—of Chekhov—the terrible monotony of Proust, of the Marquis de Sade, etc., etc. . . .

At the siege of Sebastopol, Tolstoy jumped out of the trenches and ran toward the bastion under heavy fire from the enemy. He was horribly afraid of rats, and had just seen one.

Politics can never be the subject of poetry (Goethe).

To add to the Absurd—quotation from Tolstoy as a model of illogical logic:

"If all the worldly goods for which we live, if all the delights which life, wealth, glory, honors, and power give to us are taken away by death, then these goods have no meaning. If life is not infinite, it is quite simply absurd, it is not worth living, and we must rid ourselves of it as soon as possible by committing suicide." (*Confession.*)

But, later on, Tolstoy modifies his remarks: "The existence of death compels us either to give up life of our own free will, or to change our life *in such a way as to give it a meaning that cannot be taken from it by death.*"

Fear and suffering: the most fleeting of emotions, according to Byrd. In the complete solitude of the North, he notices that the body makes just as absolute demands as the mind: *"He cannot do without* sounds, colors, and voices."

T. E. Lawrence enlisting again after the war, in the ranks, and under a false name. He must discover whether anonymity can give what greatness could not. He refuses the decorations offered to him by the king, gives his medal to his dog. Sends his manuscripts anonymously to publishers, who reject them. Motorcycle accident.

Hence the definition of A. Fabre-Luce: the superman can be recognized by the strictness with which he shuts himself up in history, and the inner liberty which he keeps toward it.

On rereading. The Notebooks of Malte Lauris Brigge. An insignificant book. The place responsible: Paris. It is a Parisian defeat. A Parisian infection that was not overcome. Ex.: "The world looks on the solitary man as an enemy." Wrong. It couldn't care less, and has every right to do so.

The only thing any good. The story of Arvers who, on his deathbed, corrects a mistake in French: "One must say 'collidor.' "

As Newton said: by thinking of it all the time.

Jean Hytier, on the dramatist: "He does what he wants on condition that he does what he must."

For Montherlant (the decay of chivalry brought about by women). Jehan de Saintré, p. 108. MA.LF.

Pierre de Larivey: [1] translator. *Les Esprits,* translation of Lorenzino de Medici—Saint-Evremond.

All the headlands of the coast look like a fleet of ships putting out to sea. The vessels of rock and azure tremble on their keels as if ready to set sail for the islands of light. The whole landscape of Oran is lifting anchor, and each day at noon it quivers with a great feeling of adventure. One morning, perhaps, we shall set out together.

As I lie in the burning heat of these immense dunes, the world seems to shrink down to no more than a cage of heat and blood. It goes no further than my body. But if a donkey brays afar off, then the dunes, the desert, and the sky fall into place. And then they lie at an infinite distance from me.

Essay on tragedy.
(1) The silence of Prometheus.
(2) The Elizabethans.
(3) Molière.
(4) The spirit of revolt.

Plague. "I want something which is just." "That is exactly what the plague is."

[1] Camus later adapted the play by Larivey and produced it at the Festival of Angers in 1953.

"The night, a 'true night,' how many men now know what it is really like? The waters and the earth, and the return of silence. 'And my soul too is a gushing fountain.' Ah, let the world sink away and be silent. Over there, above Pollensa. . . ."

Have no more to do with this empty heart—reject everything which dries it up. If the living waters are elsewhere, why stay here?

A time comes when one can no longer feel the emotion of love. The only thing left is tragedy. Living for someone or for something no longer has any meaning. Nothing seems to keep its meaning except the idea of dying for something.

A Spartan was publicly rebuked by an ephor because he had too fat a belly.

An Athenian proverb put the man who could neither read nor swim in the very lowest class of citizens.

Alcibiades, according to Plutarch: [2] "At Sparta, he was devoted to athletic exercises, was frugal and reserved; in Ionia, luxurious, gay and indolent; in Thrace, always drinking; in Thessaly, ever on horseback; and when he lived with Tissaphernes the Persian satrap, he exceeded the Persians themselves in magnificence and pomp."

The people one day applauded him, which caused Phocion to remark: "Have I said something stupid?"

[2] Plutarch is quoted in the Everyman edition translated by A. H. Clough.

Decadence! Speeches about decadence! The third century B.C. was a "decadent" century for Greece. With Euclid, Archimedes, Aristarchus, and Hipparchus, it gave the world geometry, physics, astronomy, and trigonometry.

There are still people who confuse individualism and the cult of one's own personality. They are talking about two different things: social and metaphysical reality. "You are not concentrating your efforts." To go from life to life means having no personality of your own. But to have a personality of your own is an idea which is peculiar to a certain form of civilization. Other people may find it the worst of misfortunes.

Contradiction in the modern world. In Athens, the people could really exercise their power only because they spent most of their time on politics, while slaves did all the work which still had to be done. Once slavery is abolished, everyone has to work. And it is when the European has reached the furthest extreme of proletarianization that the idea of popular sovereignty is at its strongest: the two things cannot be combined.

Only three actors in the Greek theater. The aim was not to create *a character*.

In Athens, there was nothing at all frivolous about the theater; performances took place only two or three times a year. And in Paris? And they want to go back to something dead. It is much better to create your own style of drama.

"However innocent a thing may be, men can still discover crime in it." Molière. Preface to *Tartuffe*.

Last scene of Act I of *Tartuffe:* "increases our interest and holds it in suspense": continued next Friday.

Solon creates the laws that made him famous and, in his old age, gives his work immortality through poetry.

Thucydides [3] makes Pericles say of the Athenians that they are "capable at the same time of taking risks and of estimating them beforehand."

The victorious triremes at Salamis were manned by the poorest Athenian citizens.

Cf. Cohen: "Athens had a theater worthy of the name only when she no longer had a poet worthy of bringing to life."

O. Flake on Sade: [4] "No value is stable for the man who cannot bow down before it. Sade cannot see why he

[3] Thucydides is quoted in Rex Warner's translation.

[4] Otto Flake's book on Sade was translated into French in 1933 by Pierre Klossowski. Camus devoted a long passage to discussing Sade in *The Rebel*, 1951, where he repeated the now generally accepted idea that Sade actually did very little, and argued that his work was important largely for historical and philosophical reasons, as an illustration of the dangers of a particular type of revolt.

should bow down, having long searched for such a reason in vain." According to Sade, the man who is without grace is responsible for nothing.

Cf. the mathematics of evil in *Juliette*.

"A monomaniac of revolt against fundamental law, a man who gives the same importance to the mind and to sexuality." He ends his life at Charenton, persecuted and in his right mind, making madmen perform in the plays where he directs everything: Tableau.

"He invented cruelties that he never put into practice himself and never wanted to—in order to enter into contact with great problems."

Moby Dick [5] and the symbol, pp. 120, 121, 123, 129, 173–177, 203, 209, 241, 310, 313, 339, 373, 415, 421, 452, 457, 460, 472, 485, 499, 503, 517, 520, 522.

[5] Camus probably read *Moby Dick* in the French translation by Lucien Jacques, Joan Smith, and Jean Giono published by Gallimard in 1941. If this is the case, then the page numbers refer more or less to the following episodes (page references to the Everyman edition):

120—End chap. XXX. Ahab's leg. Everyman, p. 114.
121—Beginning chap. XXXI. Everyman, p. 115.
123—Everyman, p. 117. Whether a whale is a fish.
129—Everyman, pp. 122–3. Black Fish—Narwhal.
173–7—Chap. XLI. The Whiteness of the Whale. Everyman, pp. 163–7.
203—Everyman, p. 192. "Now the advent of these outlandish strangers . . ."
209—Everyman, p. 197. Queequeg as the standard-bearer "hopelessly holding up hope in the midst of despair."
241—Chap. LIII. The *Town-Ho's* story of how the mate Radney was eaten by Moby Dick. Everyman, p. 227.
310—Everyman, p. 290. The Right Whale's Head.
313—End of chap. LXXIV. Resolution in facing death.
339—End of chap. LXXXII, beginning of chap. LXXXIII. Everyman, pp. 317–8.
373—Chap. XC. Everyman, p. 350. The smell of the *Rosebud*.
415—Chap. CIII. Everyman, pp. 393–4.

Feelings and images multiply a philosophy by ten.

In Athens, men concerned themselves with the dead only during the period of the Anthestaria. Once these were ended: "Depart, souls, the Anthestaria are over."

Originally, in Greek religion, everyone is in Hades. There are neither rewards nor punishments—similarly in Jewish religion. It is social considerations which give rise to the idea of rewards.

452—Chap. CXXII. Everyman, p. 420. The tempering of the harpoon.
457—Everyman, p. 425. The meeting with the *Bachelor*.
460—Everyman, p. 248. Beginning of chap. CXVI.
472—Everyman, pp. 438–9. Chap. CXX.
485—Everyman, p. 451. End of chap. CXXV.
499—Everyman, p. 463. Beginning of chap. CXXXI. *The Symphony*— Ahab weeps into the sea.
503—Everyman, p. 480. Moby Dick breaks Ahab's ivory leg.
520—End of chap. CXXXIII.
522—Everyman, p. 482. "I meet thee, this third time, Moby Dick."

It should be noted that there is a difference in the chapter numbers between the French translation and the Everyman edition referred to here. Thus, the French edition is consistently one chapter number ahead—so that chapter CXXXIV in the Everyman edition is chapter CXXXV in the French edition. The chapter headings here refer to the Everyman edition.

The question of Melville's influence on Camus has been raised by a number of critics, and there is an essay on "Les étrangers chez Melville" by Leon S. Roudiez in *Configuration Critique, Revue des Lettres Modernes*, 1961, nos. 64–66. Mr. Roudiez has also written a study of the particular relationship of *Moby Dick* and *The Plague* which appeared in *Symposium*, Spring 1961, pp. 30–9. Mr. Roudiez also points out that Camus wrote an essay on Melville which was published in the series *Les Ecrivains célèbres* (Paris: Mazenod; 1952). He agrees that Camus almost certainly did read the 1941 translation of *Moby Dick*, and suggests, probably rightly, that *Moby Dick* is "not a major source in the usual literary meaning of the term." This seems particularly true if Camus did, indeed, mark down only the page numbers which most interested him, since the passage where the *Jeraboam* is described as stricken with plague is not one which he noted.

404. Athens having signed the armistice with Lysander, the end of the Peloponnesian War was marked by Lysander's attack on the walls of Athens to the sound of flutes.

The striking story of Timoleon, tyrant of Syracuse (he had his father imprisoned in order to kill him as a traitor).

In certain Greek cities, in the fourth century, the following oath was taken by the oligarchs: "I shall always be an enemy of the people, and I shall advise it to do what I know will be most harmful to its interests."

The flight of Darius pursued by Alexander (293–4).

The nuptials at Susa: Alexander with 10,000 soldiers, 80 generals joins the Persians.

Demetrius Poliorcetes—sometimes on the throne, at the height of power, sometimes wandering from village to village.

Antisthenes: "It is a regal thing to do good and hear evil spoken of oneself."

Cf. Marcus Aurelius: "Wherever it is possible to live, it is possible to live well."

"What prevents a work from being completed becomes the work itself."

What bars our way makes us travel along it.

Ended February 1942

BIOGRAPHICAL NOTE

APPENDICES A AND B

BIOGRAPHICAL NOTE

11.7.13. Birth of Albert Camus at Mondovi, Constantine, French North Africa.

10.11.14. Lucien Camus, his father, is killed at the first Battle of the Marne. His mother, née Catherine Sintès, goes to live in Belcourt, a working-class suburb of Algiers. She works as a charwoman to provide for Camus and his elder brother Lucien, who are brought up largely by their maternal grandmother.

1918–1923. Camus attends the *école communale* of Belcourt. His Nobel Prize speech of 1957 is dedicated to his teacher, Louis Germain.

1923. Wins scholarship to the lycée in Algiers (now Lycée Albert Camus).

1928–1930. Is goalkeeper for the Racing Universitaire d'Alger.

1930. First attack of tuberculosis.

1933. First marriage, to Simone Hie.

1934. Joins Communist Party. Works on the Arab question. Laval's visit to Moscow in 1935 brings about a change in the Party line, and Camus begins to feel critical. He did not, however, Roger Quilliot tells me, actually leave the Party until 1937, the date at which the Théâtre du Travail, which he had been instrumental in founding, broke its Communist links and became the Théâtre de L'Equipe.

1935. Begins the *cahiers*. Completes his *licence de philosophie* (B.A.) in June. Plays an active part in the Communist *Maison de la Culture* in Algiers. Co-operates in writing *Révolte dans les Asturies,* a play about the revolt of the Oviedo miners in Spain. The play was not allowed to be publicly performed but was privately published. Begins research on Plotinus, for his *diplôme d'études supérieures* (roughly an M.A. by thesis). During the whole of this time he is supporting himself by various jobs, and works for the Institut de Météorologie.

1936. May. Successfully presents his thesis, on Néo-Platonisme et Pensée Chrétienne. Begins to work as an actor for the touring company of Radio Algiers. His first marriage is dissolved. In the summer, travels to Austria and returns via Prague and Italy.

1937. Publication of *L'Envers et L'Endroit* (written 1935–6). Compelled to go to Embrun, in France, for reasons of health in summer, and again travels back through Italy. Refuses a post as teacher in Sidi-bel-Abbès. Breaks with Communist Party.

1938. Foundation, in October, of *Alger-Républicain*, an independent left-wing paper edited by Pascal Pia. Camus joins the staff, and his first article appears on October 10, 1938. He reviews books regularly, but also writes a large number of other articles. Completes first version of *Caligula*.

1939. January–March. Series of articles in *Alger-Républicain* leading to the acquittal of Michel Hodent. July. Publication of eleven articles on Kabylia, describing the poverty of the area and criticizing government policy. The more important of these were republished in *Actuelles III* in 1938, and some were translated in *Resistance, Rebellion, and Death* in 1960.

1939. September. Camus made editor of the evening paper *Le Soir-Républicain*, where he signs a number of articles Jean Mersault. Publication of *Noces*. Rejected for military service for reasons of health.

1940. January–February. Both *Soir-Républicain* and *Alger-Républicain* cease to appear. Camus is unable to find a job in Algeria because of his political affiliations, and goes to Paris, where Pascal Pia finds him a place in *Paris-Soir*. Camus contributed no articles to this paper, which he disliked, and worked only as a type-setter.

1940. June. Leaves Paris with *Paris-Soir* and goes to Clermont-Ferrand. Then to Bordeaux and Lyons. December. Second marriage, to Francine Faure.

1941. Return to Oran. Teaches for a short time in a private school. Completes *Le Mythe de Sisyphe*. December 19. Execution of Gabriel Péri—an event which, according to Camus himself, crystallized his revolt against the Germans.

1942. Return to France. July. Publication of *L'Etranger*. Camus joins the resistance network *Combat* in the Lyons region. January. New attack of tuberculosis.

1943. Publication of *Le Mythe de Sisyphe*. First of the *Lettres à un Ami Allemand* (translated in *Resistance, Rebellion, and Death*). *Combat* sends him to Paris, where he is by now well known in literary circles. He becomes a publisher's reader and permanent member of the administrative staff at Gallimard. In order to avoid ever feeling that he had to publish books in order to earn his living, Camus kept this job until the end of his life.

1944. August. Editor of *Combat*. His unsigned, and supposedly anonymous, editorials are characteristic of the hopes and aspirations of the liberation period, and, coming after the first performance, in June 1944, of *Le Malentendu* (written 1942–1943), emphasized the dual nature of his attitude toward the world.

1945. Still with *Combat*, though writing less frequently. First performance of *Caligula*, in September, with Gérard Philipe in title role. Publication of *Lettres à un Ami Allemand* and of *La Remarque sur la Révolte*, starting point of *L'Homme Révolté*. Birth of his twin children, Catherine and Jean.

1946. Visit to America. Completion of *La Peste*.

1947. June. Publication of *La Peste*. Great success. On June 3, 1947, Camus leaves *Combat*, whose financial difficulties no longer allow an independent editorial policy.

1948. October. First performance of *L'État de Siège*.

1949. June–August. Lecture tour in South America, described in detail in the later *Notebooks*. Camus falls ill, and has to spend a long time convalescing.

1950. Publication of *Actuelles I*. Performance of *Les Justes*.

1951. *L'Homme Révolté*.

1952. Public quarrel with Sartre.

1953. Replaces Marcel Herrand as producer at the Festival d'Angers. *Actuelles II*.

1954. Publication of *L'Eté*, a collection of essays written between 1939 and 1954. Includes *Le Minotaure ou la Halte d'Oran*, many passages of which were first written in the *Carnets*. (Cf. English translation by Justin O'Brien in the volume containing the 1955 English translation of *Le Mythe de Sisyphe*.)

1955. Travels to Greece. Goes back to journalism in *L'Express* to support the election campaign of Mendès-France. Appeals for an agreement by both sides in the Algerian War to respect the civilian population.

1956. Publication of *La Chute*. Adaptation of Faulkner's *Requiem for a Nun*.

1957. Publication of the short stories *L'Exil et le Royaume*. Publication of the *Réflexions sur la Guillotine*, in a companion volume with Arthur Koestler's *Reflections on Hanging*. Awarded the Nobel Prize for Literature.

1958. Publication of *Actuelles III*. Articles on Algeria dating from 1939–58.

1959. Adaptation of Dostoevsky's *The Possessed*. Camus continues work on his projected novel *Le Premier Homme*.

1960. January 5. Killed in an automobile accident.

The two most useful studies on Camus's life are by Roger Quilliot, *La Mer et les Prisons* (Gallimard 1956), and by Germaine Brée, *Camus* (Rutgers 1959). I am indebted to M. Quilliot for additional information used both in the biographical note and in certain other notes in the *Notebooks*.

APPENDIX A

Newspaper articles published by Camus
between 1938 and 1940

A. *Alger-Républicain* (began publishing October 6, 1938)
All these articles were signed Albert Camus or A. C.

1938

10.9.38. Review of Aldous Huxley: *Those Barren Leaves*.

10.10.38. Review of Erich-Maria Remarque: *Les Camarades*.

10.11.38. Review of Blanche Balain: *La Sève des Justes*.

10.20.38. Review of Jean-Paul Sartre: *La Nausée*.

10.23.38. Jean Hytier: *André Gide*.

10.24.38. *Le point de vue de ceux qui n'ont pas voté* (account of a senatorial election in Algiers).

11.2.38. Review of René Janon: *Les Salopards*.

11.11.38 Review of Paul Nizan: *La Conspiration*.

11.19.38. *Au pays du Mufle* (defense of the International Brigade).

11.22.38. Review of Edmond Bruca: *Les Fables Bônoises*.

11.26.38. "Un vapeur français? Stoppez ou je tire . . ." (a Spanish gunboat arrests a French merchant vessel in the Mediterranean).

11.27.38. *Les Meetings d'Alger. A la bourse du travail* (account of the demonstrations against the Daladier-Reynaud laws).

11.28.38. *Revue des revues*.

12.1.38. *Ces hommes qu'on raie de l'humanité.*

12.3.38. *Dialogue entre un Président du Conseil et un employé à 1200 francs par mois.*

12.21.38. *15 municipaux seront mis à pied pendant huit jours* (protest against the suspension from their jobs of fifteen municipal employees of the town of Algiers by the mayor, Monsieur Rozis, because they took part in a strike).

12.30.38. *Une cassure dans une conduite de gaz est mise à jour rue Blanchard.*

12.31.38. *L'enquête sur l'explosion de la rue Blanchard continue dans le secret.*

1939

1.3.39. Review of Renaud de Jouvenel: *Commune Mesure.*
Jean Giono: *Le Lettre aux Paysans sur la Pauvreté et la Paix.*

1.10.39. *Lettre ouverte à Monsieur le Gouverneur Général* (Camus's first intervention on behalf of Michel Hodent, a technical agent of the Office National du Blé who had been imprisoned on a false accusation of fraud).

1.14.39. *Grâce au couscous offert par Mme Chapauton, des enfants ont pu manger.*

1.16.39. Review of Felix de Chazournes: *Caroline ou le départ pour les îles.*

1.28.39. Review of Marie Mauron: *Le Quartier Mortisson.*
Review of a lecture entitled *De la Modernité des Anciens* given by M. Louis Gernet.

2.4.39. *L'Affaire Hodent ou les caprices de la justice.*

2.5.39. Review of Henry de Montherlant: *L'Equinoxe de Septembre.*

2.7.39. *Monsieur Rozis révoque cinq employés municipaux.*

2.18.39. *Livres de Femmes.*

2.19.39. *Sur une conférence de Monsieur Claude Farrère* (very critical account of a lecture given in defense of Japanese policy in China).

2.22.39. *L'Affaire Hodent ou la multiplication des abus du pouvoir.*

3.1.39. *L'Affaire Hodent prend de l'extension.*

3.5.39. *Michel Hodent comparaîtra le 20 mars devant le tribunal correctionnel de Tiaret.*

Review of Arnaud Guibert: *Périple des îles Tunisiennes.*

Abd-Errahmann ben El-Haffaf: *Introduction à l'étude de l'Islam.*

Aimé Dupy: *Du Bled à la côte.*

3.7.39. *Depuis quand poursuit-on la conscience professionnelle?* (On Hodent.)

3.9.39. *Comment on circonvient et on éloigne un témoin gênant* (on Hodent).

3.12.39. Review of Jean-Paul Sartre: *Le Mur.*

3.13.39. *Un homme juste plaide pour un innocent* (Hodent).

3.16.39. *Les "Complices" de Michel Hodent et les fantaisies de l'instruction.*

3.18.39. *L'Affaire Hodent: Pour s'effondrer dans le ridicule, l'instruction n'en est que plus hideuse.*

3.21.39. *L'Affaire Hodent devant le tribunal correctionnel de Tiaret.*

3.23.39. *L'Innocence de Hodent et du magasinier Mas a fini par triompher.*

3.28.39. Review of Ferreira de Castro: *Forêt Vierge.*

4.7.39. *Du cirque des puces au roi de l'évasion* (an hour at the Fair of Algiers).

4.9.39. Review of Jorge Amado: *Bahia de tous les saints.*

4.16.39. *Roman d'aventures.*

4.20.39. *La situation des Nord Africains travaillant en France* (I).

4.21.39. Idem (II).

4.23.39. Idem (III).

Romans français.

4.25.39. *La situation des Nord Africains* . . . (IV).

Account of lecture by M. R. E. Charlier: *Contre L'Impérialisme.*

BIOGRAPHICAL NOTE

4.30.39. *La situation des Nord Africains* . . . (V).

5.23.39. Review of Ignazio Silone: *Le Pain et le Vin*.

André Chamson: *La Galère*.

Review of the production of Jean Cocteau's *La Machine Infernale* by the Groupe Théâtral Universitaire.

5.25.39. Account of lecture by M. R. E. Charlier: *Pas de Guerre*.

6.5.39. First of the articles on Kabylia: I. *Le Grèce en Haillons*.

6.6.39. II. *Le Dénuement*.

6.7.39. III. *Cinq enfants meurent pour avoir mangé des racines vénéneuses*.

6.8.39. IV. *Les Salaires insultants*.

6.9.39. V. *L'Habitat*.

6.10.39. VI. *L'Assistance*.

6.11.39. VII. *L'Enseignement*.

6.12.39. VIII. *Deux aspects de la vie économique kabyle: L'artisanat et l'usure*.

6.13.39. IX. *L'Avenir politique*.

6.14.39. X. *Pour vivre, la Kabylie réclame*. . . .

6.15.39. XI. *Misère de la Kabylie*. Conclusion.

6.22.39.–6.29.39. *Le Film des Débats* (account of the trial of Sheik El Okbi, acquitted of the false accusation of having organized the assassination of the Mufti of Algiers. Camus covered this trial, but did not play as important a part as in the *Affaire Michel Hodent*).

6.25.39. *Les Ecrivains et leurs critiques*.

7.4.39. Review of Georges Bernanos: *Scandale de la Vérité*.

Albert Ollivier: *La Commune*.

7.15.39. Review of Armand Guibert: *L'oiseau privé*.

7.24.39. *Livres espagnols*.

7.25.39. *L'Affaire des "incendiaires" d'Auribeau en cassation* (I). First of four articles concerning ten Moslems who were sent to prison on a false charge of having committed arson in a strike in February 1939.

7.26.39. II. *Comme au moyen âge: La torture au service des accusations*.

7.28.39. III. *Un odieux déni de justice*.

7.31.39. IV. *Des Innocents condamnés aux travaux forcés et*

222

les leurs condamnés à la misère "au nom du peuple français."

8.18.39. *De Malencontreuses poursuites* (protest against the arrest of members of the *Parti Populaire Algérien*).

B. *Le Soir-Républicain*

Camus was editor of this newspaper from the first number on September 15, 1939, to the last of January 9, 1940. He did not, however, sign many articles in it, but used pseudonyms (Mersault, Caligula, César Borgia, Ary Delman) and, occasionally, his own initials. I should like to thank Mme Camus for helping me to identify certain articles and allowing me to consult her list of articles published in *Le Soir Républicain*, which I have used to supplement my own.

Both this newspaper and *Alger-Républicain* are available at the annex of the Bibliothèque Nationale at Versailles. The library index number of *Alger-Républicain* is Gr. Fol. Jo. 1478; that of *Le Soir Républicain*, Gr. Fol. Jo. 1826. There is a delay of two or three days before the papers can be consulted in Paris.

1939

9.17.39. *La Guerre*. A. C.

9.21.39. *La France est libre* (unsigned editorial).

11.6.39. *Sous les éclairages de guerre* (a review of the press). Signed César Borgia.

11.7.39. *Un effort généreux* (unsigned editorial).

11.15.39. *Notre revue de presse.* "Ils sont sincères." Signed Ary Delman.

11.25.39. *Une Interview de Dieu le Père*. Signed Ary Delman.

11.27.39. *La Censure avec nous* (unsigned).

12.6.39. *Notre position* (unsigned).

12.12.39. *Les Conditions d'une collaboration* (unsigned).

12.14.39. *De Richelieu à Léon Blum* (unsigned).

12.16.39. *Comment aller vers un ordre nouveau* (unsigned).

12.17.39. *Défense de notre liberté.* Signed Liber.

12.18.39. *A nos lecteurs* (unsigned).

12.19.39. *Va-t-on entrer en guerre contre l'URSS?* (Unsigned.)

12.23.39. *Lettre à un Jeune Anglais sur l'état d'esprit du peuple français.* Signed Jean Mersault.

12.30.39. *Recherche du Possible* (unsigned).

1940

1.1.40. *Le Soir Républicain* (unsigned editorial).

1.3.40. *Caligula* (remarks on censorship).

APPENDIX B

Plays performed by the Théâtre du Travail, later the Théâtre de l'Equipe, between 1935 and 1939.

André Malraux: *Le Temps du Mépris.* Camus's own adaptation.

Charles Vildrac: *Le Paquebot "Tenacity."*

André Gide: *Le Retour de l'enfant prodigue.* Camus in the title role.

Ben Jonson: *The Silent Woman.*

Aeschylus: *Prometheus Bound.* Camus's adaptation.

Dostoevsky: *The Brothers Karamazov.* Adaptation by Jacques Copeau. Camus played the part of Ivan.

Pushkin: *The Stone Guest,* or *Don Juan.*

Gorki: *The Lower Depths.*

Fernando de Rojas: *La Celestina.* Directed by Camus.

John Synge: *The Playboy of the Western World.*

The Théâtre de l'Equipe consisted entirely of amateurs who seemed, to judge from the occasional reviews of their productions in *Alger-Républicain,* to perform anonymously. The information about the parts played by Camus is taken from the studies of Roger Quilliot and Germaine Brée.

A Note on the Type

THE TEXT of this book was set on the Linotype in a face called PRIMER, designed by *Rudolph Ruzicka*, earlier responsible for the design of Fairfield and Fairfield Medium, Linotype faces whose virtues have for some time now been accorded wide recognition. The complete range of sizes of Primer was first made available in 1954, although the pilot size of 12 point was ready as early as 1951. The design of the face makes general reference to Linotype Century (long a serviceable type, totally lacking in manner or frills of any kind) but brilliantly corrects the characterless quality of that face.

Composed by Kingsport Press, Inc.,
Kingsport, Tennessee.
Printed by The Murray Printing Company,
Forge Village, Massachusetts.
Bound by H. Wolff, New York.
Typography and binding design by
GEORGE SALTER